CONTENTS

DISCA D0274002

PART ONE
INTRODUCTION

PART TWO
THE TEXT

PART THREE
CRITICAL APPROACHES

PART FOUR
CRITICAL PERSPECTIVES

PART FIVE
BACKGROUND

satisfying, and the theatre a medium rich in the potential to change society – although, especially in Britain, censorship meant that it was the private, subscription-only theatres that exploited this potential. Characters such as Nora not only embodied the situation of women, they offered what Shaw called 'vivid and solar roles' (*The Quintessence of Ibsenism*, 1932 edition, p. 60) for actresses in which they could distinguish themselves and develop their talents.

It would be too simplistic to call Ibsen a true 'Ibsenite'. While *A Doll's House* and his other plays from this period certainly fit Shaw's sense of the word with their realism and passion for social justice, Ibsen was a perpetual innovator. By the time *A Doll's House* was causing a sensation in Britain and America he was over sixty and writing in a theatrical style that can hardly be described as naturalistic. His earlier work had also had very different aims, exploring Norwegian history and myth; his first real masterpieces, *Brand* (1866) and *Peer Gynt* (1867), were poetic and explicitly Scandinavian epics, written to be read rather than acted, with spectacular scenes that challenge theatre technology to the limit (although they have been successfully staged). The success of his first markedly naturalistic play, *The Pillars of Society*, in 1877 made it inevitable that he would work in the same style for *A Doll's House*; and other naturalistic plays followed, including *Ghosts* (1881) – which shocked all of Europe – and his powerful study of a woman trapped in a loveless marriage, *Hedda Gabler* (1890). His later plays, such as *Little Eyolf* (1894) and his final work, *When We Dead Awaken* (1899), show less interest in the detailed characterisation associated with naturalism; characters seem to embody states of mind rather than emerging as products of their political or social environment.

However, Ibsen himself claimed in the preface to the first Dano-Norwegian edition of his complete works that all his writings were 'one, coherent and continuous whole' and that readers should therefore work their way through the lot in chronological order (quoted in Toril Moi's *Henrik Ibsen and the Birth of Modernism: Art, Theater, Philosophy*, 2006, p. 11). The suggestion is a little daunting: he wrote twenty-six plays and a quantity of poems. But it can be illuminating to read *A Doll's House* as the work of

 CHECK THE NET

The Theatre Museum has an excellent online guided tour to the theatre of many periods, including photographs, posters, biographies, reviews and audio clips. To begin with Ibsen and his own times, go to **www. peopleplayuk. org.uk** and click on 'Guided Tours', then 'Drama' and '19th Century Theatre'.

CONTEXT

This collected works was published in 1898 to mark the dramatist's seventieth birthday.

a specifically Norwegian writer whose early plays had been composed to establish a Norwegian national theatre. Although Nora's situation struck a chord with women across Europe, the **imagery** on which she dwells when contemplating suicide – the dark and icy waters giving up their dead in the spring thaw (Act 2, p. 200) – situates the play very precisely in the Norwegian landscape. So does her moving conversation with Dr Rank in Act 2, in which their mutual sorrow and affection are reflected by Ibsen's attention to lighting; he sets it in the growing darkness of a wintry day in the far north, when night draws in soon after noon.

It is also helpful to see Ibsen as a **symbolic** writer; the later plays make this clear with effects as spectacular as any **melodrama**: for example the great avalanche of *When We Dead Awaken*, which both kills the troubled lovers and joins them in a mystical union. Nora's tarantella, though a perfectly plausible action in a play of ordinary bourgeois life, works at a similar symbolic level. The actress reveals Nora's inner conflict through the wildness of her dance, allowing the expression of feelings she is forced to keep hidden; but it also offers the audience a sharply eloquent image of male pride and dominance. Nora is an object, a work of art for her husband to stare at and enjoy.

Ibsen liked to think of his plays as conducting a dialogue with one another – so that, for example, after showing Nora leaving her unsatisfactory marriage in *A Doll's House*, he explored in his next play, *Ghosts*, the consequences of staying: loneliness, disease and emotional sterility. It is perhaps this willingness to explore situations from so many different perspectives that gives his work its vitality. *A Doll's House* is concerned not just with the status of women but with the damage all society does to itself by refusing them equality with men. And it is also the **tragedy** of a particular marriage. It is, literally, about a 'house' full of people whose lives are changed by Nora's personal journey – her friends, her husband, her children, even her maid. The open-ended conclusion was shocking to nineteenth-century spectators conditioned to expect definite and moralistic closure. But it allows the actors considerable freedom. Readers or performers can decide, for example, whether Nora already resents having to play the 'skylark' for Helmer from the

CHECK THE BOOK
In Act 2 of Oscar Wilde's 1895 **comedy** *The Importance of Being Earnest* the governess, Miss Prism, outlines this expectation to her pupil: 'The good ended happily, and the bad unhappily. That is what Fiction means.'

outset or whether this becomes harder as Christmas wears on, and how far Helmer is unaware of his emotional dependence on his wife; they may consider how well the couple are equipped for their new future apart at the end. Every answer will be different, and most will lead to a plausible and lively version of the play.

This richness and potential for the performer has made *A Doll's House* Ibsen's most popular play. It has been staged at times of social or cultural upheaval: it was performed in Russia on the edge of the 1906 bourgeois revolution; in 1935 a production in Shanghai marked the beginning of **realistic** theatre in China. In Japan the first Nora was also the first actress in a previously all-male theatre. Even in contexts where the question of women's rights is not paramount, the freedom of interpretation it allows generates new readings in new styles. You can always find something fresh to say or to show about *A Doll's House*. Ibsen knew he had written something unique. 'I cannot remember any work of mine', he wrote to his publisher, 'that gave me so much satisfaction during the working out of the details as this one has' (quoted in Joan Templeton, *Ibsen's Women*, 2001, p. 145).

CONTEXT

In the 1920s *A Doll's House* was banned in China. Jiang Qing (1914–91), later the third wife of Mao Zedong, was an advocate of rights for women – such as the right not to have their feet bound when young – and made her name as Nora in the 1935 production seen as the beginning of cultural modernity in China.

THE TEXT

NOTE ON THE TEXT

The edition used in these Notes is the 1965 Penguin Classics edition *A Doll's House and Other Plays* translated by Peter Watts (and reprinted numerous times).

SYNOPSIS

CHECK THE FILM

Bryan Forbes's 1975 film of Ira Levin's 1972 novel *The Stepford Wives* shows a community in which the men have replaced their wives with robot imitations who flatter their egos, keep their houses looking perfect and never think for themselves. The film was remade in 2004, starring Nicole Kidman.

The play begins on Christmas Eve as a young woman, Nora Helmer, arrives home with the Christmas tree and presents for the family. She nibbles some macaroons until her husband, Torvald, comes out to greet her. He is concerned about her extravagance but she points out that his new job as manager of the local bank carries a high salary. She asks him for money as her own Christmas present. He is reluctant, calling her a spendthrift, and asks her if she has been eating sweets, which she denies.

Their conversation is interrupted by the announcement of two visitors. As (Torvald) Helmer returns to his study to greet Dr Rank, a family friend, the other caller appears – Mrs Linde, an old friend of Nora's who has fallen on hard times and hopes Nora may use her influence with Helmer to procure her a job at the bank. As Mrs Linde compares her struggle to make ends meet after the death of her unloved husband with Nora's easy life, Nora claims that she too has struggled. Helmer nearly died from overwork and they spent a year in Italy for his health. He was unwilling to pay for a trip and the doctors would not allow him to be told of the gravity of his condition; hence Nora raised the money herself, pretending it was a gift from her father, and has been secretly working to pay off the loan.

Another visitor arrives: Nils Krogstad, who has a post at the bank, and whose presence troubles Nora, although he has come to see her husband. Dr Rank appears from the study to allow Krogstad to talk privately with Helmer, and Nora introduces him to Mrs Linde. They discuss 'moral invalid[s]' (p. 165) like Krogstad and how they should be treated. Nora becomes excited that Helmer has power over Krogstad and passes round the macaroons, saying they were a present from Mrs Linde. Helmer returns and is glad to offer Mrs Linde a job. He goes out with her and Rank, while Nora plays with her children, but she is interrupted by Krogstad. Threatened with dismissal from the bank, he has come to blackmail Nora into using her influence to help him. It emerges that he was the source of the loan – and Nora forged her father's signature in order to guarantee it. If she does not get him his job back, he will reveal everything.

Helmer returns in time to see Krogstad leaving. Assuming he has come to play on Nora's goodwill, and angry when she tries to deny it, Helmer pronounces that liars like Krogstad – and, even worse, 'lying mothers' (p. 179) – damage their children. Alone again, Nora is deeply troubled; she tells their nursemaid that she does not want to see her children.

Act 2 begins on Christmas Day, the tree already stripped of its presents. Nora is still troubled. The nurse arrives with her outfit for the fancy dress party she and Helmer are attending that night; Nora will not see her children, and asks the nurse how it felt when she left her own baby to look after Nora. Mrs Linde arrives, and begins to mend the costume. She asks about Dr Rank, wondering if he is the source of the loan, only to be bundled out of the room as Helmer arrives – he does not like to watch dressmaking. Nora tries to intercede for Krogstad. Helmer becomes angry, recalling the shoddy reputation of Nora's father; and finally, in a fit of petulance, sends Krogstad a letter of dismissal. Nora panics and pleads with him to change his mind; he patronisingly promises that he is 'man enough' (p. 190) to deal with any trouble, before retiring to his study.

Dr Rank arrives; he has come to tell Nora that he is dying. He and Nora discuss his illness, syphilis, in an elaborate code and start to flirt over the silk stockings she will wear to the party. Nora has just begun to sound him out for help over the loan, when he declares his love for her; she reproves him and refuses to go on with her request, sending him to visit Helmer just as Krogstad arrives. Furious at his

CONTEXT

The relationship between crime and sickness was hotly debated during the nineteenth century. Those who subscribed to Darwin's theory of evolution, for example, might have seen the criminal as an unhealthy specimen doomed to die out, rather than as a person with sole responsibility for his actions.

 CHECK THE BOOK

The idea of moral invalidity is **satirically** explored in *Erewhon* (1872), a novel by Ibsen's contemporary Samuel Butler (1835–1902). In this imaginary state (an anagram of 'nowhere') the sick are treated as criminals and those who commit crimes are cared for as if they are ill.

CHECK THE NET

Ibsen.net –
www.ibsen.net –
was launched in
2002 in three
languages. On it
you can find in-
depth information
and articles about
Ibsen, including all
his own paintings,
details of
productions
worldwide and links
to major museums.
There are also
quotations and
quizzes, and a
regularly updated
calendar of Ibsen
events.

CHECK THE BOOK

*The Cambridge
Companion to
Ibsen*, edited by
James McFarlane
(1994), is a useful
general
introduction and
contains essays
on major aspects
of Ibsen's plays,
together with
a detailed
bibliography.

dismissal, Krogstad informs her he now wants a better job. Panicking, Nora thinks of suicide. Krogstad leaves a note in the locked letter box telling Helmer everything.

Mrs Linde arrives and Nora confides in her; Mrs Linde thinks the truth should come out, but offers to go and speak to Krogstad, who once cared for her. Nora talks wildly and confusingly about a 'miracle' that must be prevented; as Helmer and Rank emerge from the study, she pleads with her husband not to open the mail and persuades him to help her rehearse the tarantella she will perform at the party. Mrs Linde returns, informing her that Krogstad is out of town. Nora tells herself she has 'thirty-one hours to live' (p. 206) and rushes into Helmer's arms as the curtain falls.

As Act 3 begins Mrs Linde is waiting at the Helmers' house while the party is going on upstairs. Krogstad arrives; it emerges that Mrs Linde ended the relationship to marry a wealthier man in order to support her mother and brothers. Krogstad feels that his life is like a shipwreck, his only comfort the job he has lost – to her. She proposes that they 'join forces' (p. 209). She wants to work and care for him and his children, and has faith he can do better. He is sceptical that she wants only a favour for Nora, but when he accepts that she cares for him and offers to take his letter back, she tells him that the truth must come out for the sake of Nora and Helmer.

Krogstad leaves, and the Helmers return. Helmer feels the tarantella has been a great success and, after a slightly drunken lecture to Mrs Linde about the merits of embroidery versus knitting, is glad to show her out. He wants to make love to a troubled Nora, but they are interrupted by Dr Rank – who ostensibly wants only a cigar, but who tells Nora in code that he has performed the last test on himself and confirmed the final stage of the disease has begun. As he leaves he puts two calling cards marked with a black cross in the letter box. Nora explains their meaning to Helmer, who continues his unwelcome attentions until she reproaches him for his insensitivity. She tells him to read his letters. As he reads the one from Krogstad he erupts in a rage, and informs her that their marriage is over – although they will preserve a front for the sake of respectability.

The maid arrives with another letter. It is from Krogstad, returning the paper with the forged signature and promising no further action. Helmer selfishly rejoices that he is saved, while Nora is lost in profound disillusionment. As she takes off her fancy dress, Helmer lectures her about the depth of his forgiveness. She emerges in day clothes, to demand the first serious talk of their lives. She accuses him and her father of denying her the chance to grow up, and says she is leaving him to educate herself: a 'duty' higher than that of wife or mother (p. 228). When he realises that she has ceased to love him, she explains the 'miracle' she was expecting – that he would step forward to take all the blame. When he failed, she felt she was married to a 'strange man' (p. 230). She feels she must go, and, as Helmer pleads with her, says that she could only return if they both changed and their relationship became 'a real marriage' (p. 232). As she leaves, the door slams behind her.

DETAILED SUMMARIES

ACT 1

PAGES 147–53

- Nora Helmer arrives home with her Christmas shopping.
- Nora and her husband, Torvald, discuss household expenses.
- He teases her about eating sweets as visitors arrive.

The curtain rises on a middle-class, nineteenth-century home of modest prosperity. The bell rings and Nora Helmer enters, laden with Christmas parcels and followed by a porter carrying a Christmas tree. Happy and excited as she arranges for the tree to be hidden from her children, she nibbles at some macaroons she has bought. Her husband calls from his study; she hides the macaroons and invites him out, but he chats with the closed door between them until she mentions spending money; then he comes out and reminds her that although he will soon have a better salary, it hasn't started

CONTEXT

Nora's idea of wrapping up some banknotes in 'pretty gold paper' (p. 150) is like the running joke between Ibsen and his wife, Suzannah. He would make elaborately decorated 'banknotes' for her from the 'National Bank of Ibsen', which he replaced with real money when he had sold some of his work. Several of these have survived.

yet. He is concerned about getting into debt. He asks Nora what she wants for Christmas and she asks him for money; he teases her for extravagance and goes on to ask her if she has been eating sweets, which she denies. He reflects on how well he is doing – this year there will be a dinner with fine wine and a guest, their friend Dr Rank. He recalls the previous Christmas when they had to struggle and Nora's efforts at making decorations came to nothing. Nora has something she wants to tell him, but they are interrupted as the maid announces visitors.

COMMENTARY

Ibsen's title suggests the location is important, and while Nora is making her way upstairs the audience is able to observe the 'house' without the characters. Stage **naturalism** – the representation of plausible situations on sets designed to look as **realistic** as possible – was still relatively new in 1879 and this is only Ibsen's second play of contemporary life. The upper-middle-class room would have been novel for his first audience, used to more aristocratic locations for drama, and they would have responded to clues already visible. This is a household with pretensions to culture – the engravings point to an interest in art. The piano, an expensive item of furniture, suggests a reasonable prosperity, as does Nora's Christmas tree a little later. Although Norway is a land of pine forests, this was a luxury item for Scandinavian families of the period.

The audience might also have expectations on observing that the room has four doors. Popular drama of the period depended on intrigue, and so many entrances to a single living room suggests this will feature in the plot: in fact, doors will be a key image. The bell that rings before Nora's entrance is a clue that she does not possess her own key. Her first word is 'Hide'. The festive tree, her high spirits and her generosity to the porter imply that this will be a domestic **comedy** and its intrigues light-hearted. This is reinforced by the first real laugh. Helmer has no intention of leaving his study till he registers the word 'bought' (p. 148), which brings him popping out like a bird from a cuckoo clock. This is a variation on a comic device, the **double take**, where someone briefly ignores important information before shock suddenly dawns; the laughter springs from the actor's rapid change of expression. Here his rush to

CONTEXT

One of the engravings (or etchings) prominent on the set of the first production was a copy of Raphael's *Sistine Madonna* (c.1512–14), a painting that the Helmers might have encountered on their Italian holiday. This offers a visual image of the perfect woman and mother Nora is expected to be.

WWW. CHECK THE NET

To view this painting by Raphael, visit the Web Gallery of Art at **www.wga.hu** and search for the title and 'Raffaello Sanzio'.

the door marks Helmer as a potential figure of fun, fussy about money. However, there seems to be no threat of poverty.

The difference in male and female attitudes to spending is at the level of comedic stereotyping still evident in the more old-fashioned kind of TV sitcom. Helmer's names for his wife – 'skylark' and 'squirrel' (p. 148) – may sound patronising, and she has no nickname for him; however, her line 'if you only knew what expenses we skylarks and squirrels have' (p. 151) suggests the animal names are a private joke in a happy relationship. If Helmer labours the point that Nora is impractical – he derides her attempts to make Christmas decorations – this is consistent with a light comedy about a dizzy young wife with a sensible husband. Indeed, Ibsen's first Nora, Betty Hennings, was famous for this kind of role.

However, there are indications of deeper issues beneath the comic surface. Not only is Nora without a key, her reluctance to open or knock on Helmer's door implies that she does not have access to all of her house. And while Helmer's interrogation about cakes seems playful – any husband might tease a wife breaking her diet – the line 'you've given me your word' (p. 152) suggests a disturbing lack of trust.

CONTEXT

American situation comedies of the 1950s such as *I Love Lucy* or *Father Knows Best* operated on the premise that a woman's place was in the home – even if she sometimes tried to work or explore the world, she would make a mess of it. Generally shot on a single set (the house), these sitcoms would often open with the husband arriving back from work shouting, 'Honey, I'm home!'

GLOSSARY

147	***stove*** this was a prominent feature of a nineteenth-century Scandinavian living room; in the play it is like the heart of the house, as the stage directions frequently demand that Nora go to warm herself on or replenish it
	øre … krone Swedish currency, coming into use all over Scandinavia at the time of the play. A krone would be worth about 10p – then a substantial tip (there are 100 øre in a krone)
149	**dress-lengths** enough material with which to make a dress; a common present for a maid
150	**ducks-and-drakes** from the old-fashioned English expression 'to play ducks and drakes' with money, i.e. to squander it. There is no exact equivalent to the word Ibsen uses, *spillefugl* ('playbird'), which is the slang for a gambler

PAGES 153–64

- Mrs Linde asks Nora to use her influence with Helmer to get her a job.
- Nora tells Mrs Linde her secret.
- Krogstad comes to see Helmer.

The visitors – Mrs Linde and Dr Rank – are shown in. Helmer goes to his study to meet Dr Rank, and Nora is left to entertain her old friend Kristina Linde, newly arrived in town. Mrs Linde mentions her widowhood, and Nora is surprised that she does not feel any loss or sorrow. She contrasts this with her own luck, telling Mrs Linde that Helmer has been made manager of the bank. Their financial worries are over – although Nora stresses that things have not always been easy. When Helmer became ill from overwork she organised an extended holiday abroad which saved his life.

Mrs Linde has been desperately poor and is lonely now her brothers have left home. She hopes Nora can persuade Helmer to offer her a job at the bank; when Nora agrees, Mrs Linde makes a comment about receiving such kindness from someone knowing 'so little about the troubles and hardships of life' (p. 158). Piqued, Nora reveals a secret: she raised the money for Helmer's year abroad. She teases Mrs Linde with the idea that it might have come from an admirer, then explains that she borrowed it and has been paying off the loan by strict economy and working in secret as a copy clerk. The extra money has come as a great relief.

A man called Krogstad enters and seems to disconcert Nora, although he asks to speak to Helmer. As he enters the study Mrs Linde is curious. Told his name by Nora, she says that she used to know him. Nora seems keen to dismiss the subject.

COMMENTARY

Initially, the two female characters are sharply contrasted. Although they were at school together, Mrs Linde looks older. We can infer

CONTEXT

The typewriter was not yet in widespread use as early models tended to jam (the first reasonably successful machine was produced by the gunmakers E. Remington & Sons in Ilion, New York, from 1874 to 1878). Important documents requiring multiple copies were hand-copied by clerks – this is the work that Nora is doing. It would not be a very well-paid job, although it requires some intelligence if mistakes are to be avoided.

that her clothes show she is poor, and a widow – nineteenth-century mourning conventions were strict and it is likely that she would wear shabby black or grey. She makes a contrast to Nora – her rather envious remarks suggest she considers Nora stylishly dressed – although we will learn that there is a secret behind the elegant dress, and clothes will have an important role in the play. Mrs Linde's garments also indicate that she has been travelling, while the housewifely Nora fusses about chairs and – as she often does – gravitates to the stove, the source of domestic warmth and comfort. Mrs Linde's function in the scene is a traditional one – she is a confidante whose function is to listen to the heroine's secrets. However, Ibsen gives her a more active role: she has her own story. Not only has she faced the poverty and bereavement with which Helmer jokingly threatens Nora, she values work for its own sake. This makes her a mirror in which Nora can view herself, not as what she is but as what she could become.

CHECK THE BOOK

The play within a play in *The Critic*, Richard Sheridan's 1779 **comedy** about the theatre, famously contains the line 'Enter Tilburina stark mad in white satin, and her confidante stark mad in white linen.'

The ensuing revelations change our understanding of Nora. We see she is competent at handling money, and the silliness she assumes in cajoling money from Helmer is a conscious performance; she may even look different to us, as we re-evaluate her attractive clothes as bargains rather than extravagances. Two of her confidences to Mrs Linde suggest that Nora's own image of herself is undergoing alterations: Nora can envisage a time when Helmer is tired of her; she has also greatly enjoyed earning money, 'like being a man' (p. 162). But we also change our view of Helmer. It is to Nora the doctors turned to explain his condition: Helmer lacked the strength of character to deal with such information and she does not think his pride could cope with financial dependency on her. We also re-evaluate the house itself as a place of secrets as well as happiness.

GLOSSARY

153	**steamer** paddle steamers, the most common mode of transport in a country that is long and narrow with an irregular coastline
156	**dollars** specie dollars, the former national currency replaced by the krone in 1875 but still in use at the time of the play

PAGES 164–9

CONTEXT

Today 'macaroon' is used to describe several kinds of sweet cakes and biscuits, but here it refers to a small delicacy based on ground almonds and egg white very fashionable in Paris. Traditionally they originated in an Italian monastery in the late eighteenth century and were brought to France by Carmelite nuns who supported themselves during the French Revolution by selling them. They are hard to make and thus expensive – perhaps the real reason Helmer forbids them.

- Dr Rank, Mrs Linde and Nora discuss Krogstad and corruption.
- Helmer offers Mrs Linde a job.
- Nora plays with her children and then receives a shock.

Dr Rank slips out of the study and Nora introduces him to Mrs Linde. Mrs Linde mentions her exhaustion and the conversation turns to moral health: Rank describes Krogstad as a 'moral invalid' (p. 165). Nora becomes cheerful, reflecting that Helmer has 'power over so many people' (p. 166), and offers them the macaroons – which, she says, Mrs Linde has brought, unaware of Helmer's ban on sweets. She silences Dr Rank by stuffing one in his mouth. She becomes almost boisterous, saying she longs to swear in front of Helmer; however, when her husband enters she persuades him to employ Mrs Linde in the coy childish tone she adopted previously.

Helmer and the visitors leave as the nurse brings back Nora's children from playing in the snow. Nora begins a game of hide-and-seek, but is interrupted by the entrance of Krogstad.

COMMENTARY

After the quiet **duologues** the stage is suddenly busy. The arrivals and departures seem at first to have little dramatic purpose beyond prolonging **suspense**: the audience is curious to know why Nora is uncomfortable at the presence of Krogstad and she is clearly not going to explain this to her guests. However, a theme is emerging: that of responsibility. Dr Rank and Mrs Linde conduct a short debate which uses Krogstad as an example: should a responsible society tolerate his moral weakness and give him a chance to redeem himself through honest work? Or does this merely deprive a better man of a job?

 CHECK THE NET

Find out how to make your own macaroons at **www.timesonline. co.uk** – search for 'macaroons'.

Nora claims to be bored by this rather abstract discussion. However, as she starts to distribute macaroons, her guests are confronted with a dilemma: will they take responsibility for telling Helmer about the forbidden sweets, or will they conceal the truth? Despite the upright tone of their debate, both of them gobble the macaroons and keep quiet. This tiny comic moment suggests that taking responsibility for one's actions, or owning up to a lie, is not easy. (Helmer will shortly hold forth about Krogstad's failure to 'freely' confess his guilt (Act 1, p. 179) as if it were a simple matter.) Nora's greed – 'just a little one. Or two at the most' (p. 166) – is funny, and her sudden urge to swear makes her amusingly like a child with a sugar rush. However, excessive eating can also be a symptom of suppressed rage. Nora never does swear in front of Helmer – but perhaps here she is symbolically 'eating her words' instead.

The arrival of the children opens up the question of responsibility to the family. While fathers of the period had less engagement with childcare than today, Helmer seems comically anxious to offload them, hastening off with 'this is no place for anyone but a mother!' (p. 168). Nora, on the other hand, is keen to be with them, dancing with them, cuddling them and taking off their wet things. This reflects her childlike nature; but at the same time, her concern for the nurse's comfort shows her to be a considerate employer. Ibsen's lines and detailed stage directions should be taken as a series of cues for the actress to improvise with the children; they allow her to give an impression of ease and spontaneity, indicating that Nora is a devoted and practised mother rather than simply indulging a whim.

 QUESTION

In an interview with the magazine *Woman's Own* Margaret Thatcher stated: 'There is no such thing as society. There are individual men and women and there are families' (31 October 1987). Is this Nora's view? Does it undergo any change in the course of the play?

 CHECK THE BOOK

Susie Orbach's *Fat Is a Feminist Issue* (1979) was the first popular text to explore in detail the complex relationship between women and food and suggest that both excessive consumption and excessive dieting have their roots in troubled relationships, the changing shape of the body graphically dramatising what the sufferer is not willing or able to say in words.

GLOSSARY

167   telegram a relatively new means of communication at the time, telegraphy was used for speed and urgency. Mrs Linde has been very prompt in visiting Nora in the hope of securing a job

PAGES 169–77

- Krogstad is revealed as the moneylender.
- He asks Nora to use her influence with her husband to help him keep his job, and threatens to tell Helmer what she has done.
- We learn that Nora forged her father's signature on the IOU.

Krogstad slips into the room unseen, frightening Nora, who hustles her children out. She is surprised that he wants to see her – she pays him on the first of the month. He asks her about Mrs Linde, mentioning that he once knew her; Nora boasts that she got Mrs Linde the post at the bank, and demands more respect. He replies that he is about to lose his own job and 'advise[s]' her to use her influence (p. 171). She refuses. He explains that he 'got into trouble' in the past and the position has allowed him to make a respectable living again (p. 172).

Nora assumes he is threatening only her relationship with Helmer and challenges him to tell the truth. Krogstad leads her to admit that she forged her father's name as guarantor of the loan; Nora says she wanted to save him worry on his deathbed and is horrified at Krogstad's claim that she is as guilty as he once was and equally liable to prosecution. With this clear but unspoken threat, Krogstad leaves. Nora feels unable to continue the game with her children and begins to decorate the Christmas tree.

COMMENTARY

Blackmail, compromising documents and villainous moneylenders were the stock-in-trade of the prolific playwright Eugène Scribe (1791–1861), popular throughout nineteenth-century Europe; he coined the term *pièce bien faite* (**well-made play**) to describe the structure he had devised to maximise the thrills, and discipline the often very extravagant and emotional style, of the drama of his time. Ibsen directed dozens of these plays and, though he despised them, Krogstad's sudden entry after tantalising hints shows the same

CONTEXT

Scribe's first play appeared in 1815; he wrote at least five hundred during his lifetime. His disciple Victorien Sardou (1831–1908) developed the well-made play format and it was enormously influential in the theatre of the nineteenth century. Their plays are virtually unknown now – except for a version of one of Sardou's works, which is played all over the world as the opera *Tosca*.

adroit manipulation of suspense. However, the tone of this scene is different; there are no heroes or villains, but complex and fallible characters. Nora reveals a snobbish discourtesy towards Krogstad as a member of an inferior class: 'one of my husband's subordinates' (p. 170). She tells the children he is a 'strange man' (p. 170); we have already heard Helmer lecture her about paying one's creditors, and her response: 'Who bothers about them? They're just strangers' (p. 149). The compassion she has shown to Mrs Linde, Dr Rank and the nurse is instinctive, not a principle she applies to the world at large – as she says, 'What do I care for your dreary old community?' (p. 165). Krogstad's reminder of their arrangement is a deft piece of exposition which provides us with important information; however, the painstaking way he takes her through the story step by step also helps us to realise that her horizons have been narrowed by her upbringing – she genuinely believes that motive is as important as legality.

While Krogstad is implacable, he is also desperate. Blackmailers in well-made plays of the period demanded large sums of money, or sex, from the helpless heroine; all Krogstad wants is respectability – in fact, ironically enough, he wants to be just like Helmer. He tries to make clear to Nora that she has committed a crime; his hint that he did 'nothing more – and nothing worse' (p. 175) suggests that, like Mrs Linde, Krogstad is a mirror in which Nora can view herself: if the independent woman showed her what she could become, Krogstad is the scared and deceitful criminal she will be if she does not face her problem. It is not surprising that his exit prompts a flurry of activity on Nora's part. She decorates the Christmas tree not only to distract herself from anxiety, but to perform the role of the pretty and carefree wife Helmer wants her to be.

CHECK THE POEM

The poem 'In Autumn' was Ibsen's first piece of writing to appear in print; it was published in the *Kristiania Post* on 28 September 1849 under the pseudonym Brynjolf Bjarme – the name under which his first plays *Catiline* and *The Warrior's Barrow* appeared in the following year.

GLOSSARY

173   **note of hand** a handwritten promise to pay an amount of money in the future, legally binding; also known as an IOU ('I owe you ...')

PAGES 177–80

- Helmer lectures Nora for lying and she diverts him with talk of the coming party.
- Helmer explains that Krogstad will corrupt his own children.
- Nora refuses to see her children.

Helmer returns and at once challenges Nora about Krogstad's visit. When she tries to deny it, he lectures her about lying. Nora changes the subject to the coming fancy dress party and asks his advice on what to wear, but she cannot help returning to the subject of Krogstad. Helmer tells her that Krogstad was a forger, and that he tried to lie his way out of the situation. This Helmer regards as the unforgivable act, explaining that deceit corrupts the family of the deceiver. Nora is shaken, especially when Helmer begins to generalise from his experience of the law, saying that most young criminals have 'lying mothers' (p. 179). As he retires to his study Nora is in a state of near panic, and when the nurse asks to enter with the children she refuses to let them come near her.

CONTEXT

While Helmer chooses small and vulnerable creatures often imprisoned in cages as nicknames for Nora, Ibsen's nicknames for his wife, Suzannah, were the more independent 'eagle' and 'cat'. (Some of Ibsen's friends considered that he himself looked like an angry badger.)

COMMENTARY

Helmer's entry comes as a surprise, just as Krogstad's did; the space is beginning to resemble a trap in which Nora is helpless. His questions reinforce this impression; he clearly knows that Krogstad has been there. As he continues to pressure Nora, she even admits things that are not the case: Krogstad did *not* ask her to conceal his visit. Helmer seems more anxious to put Nora in the wrong than to think about Krogstad. His use of the 'songbird' image (p. 177) stresses her status as a pet – and as a creature in a cage – underlining the idea that a submissive and therefore truthful wife is an important part of the furniture of his peaceful home.

The way Nora weaves the subject of Krogstad in and out of a discussion of her projected fancy dress is interesting. She begins the conversation about the party as a topic that will please and distract Helmer. However, the line 'Everything seems so stupid and pointless' (p. 178) suggests that she is offering him a cue to enter a different conversation – perhaps about Krogstad, perhaps about what she has been doing, or perhaps even about wider issues raised by Dr Rank and Mrs Linde. Whatever her intent, Helmer crushes it with his patronising reply: 'So little Nora's realized that?' As Helmer reveals his radical strategy to reorganise the bank, we see her realise something else – that Krogstad too is under pressure. Her 'poor Krogstad' may reflect dawning compassion for the 'stranger', as well as an attempt to influence her husband (p. 178).

CHECK THE BOOK

In *Drama from Ibsen to Brecht* (1976) Raymond Williams discusses the implications of showing the 'real' world on stage, and considers that the best naturalistic drama makes it clear that these ordinary conversations and objects are 'a counterpoint to the unrealised life – the inner and common desires, fears, possibilities – which struggles to find itself in just this solidly staged world' (p. 180).

Nora's instant switch to the topic of fancy dress at Helmer's 'Hm!' suggests that she has had a great deal of practice in manipulating her husband and will know exactly the right moment to return to Krogstad. The **irony** of Helmer's talk about liars shows Ibsen handling with great assurance one of the developing conventions of **naturalistic** theatre: apparently casual words spoken by one character which have a devastating effect on another. From Helmer's viewpoint, his remark is just an opportunity to show off his skill in argument, which he expects Nora to admire. She, however, fresh from the debate between Dr Rank and Mrs Linde, is genuinely afraid that she could corrupt her children. Ibsen's stage direction tells the actress playing Nora to come '*closer behind him*' (p. 179) – hence her husband cannot see the look on her face, but we can.

Helmer then effectively manipulates Nora into promising that she will drop the subject; by forcing her to shake hands, he is making her give her word to do so. He has previously made her give her word not to eat sweets (p. 152). It seems that he expects to control her behaviour in serious as well as trivial matters. Nora, however, is physically and mentally agitated, complaining how 'hot' it is (p. 180). When she refuses to allow the nurse to bring the children in to see her, it is clear that Nora is now not just afraid of what Krogstad may do; she is afraid of herself.

As the curtain falls, the audience will not only wonder how the blackmail plot will play out, but how this woman who has already begun to change will deal with the new and frightening idea that her crime may have made her an unfit mother for her children.

ACT 2

PAGES 181–6

- Nora asks her old nurse whether she misses her own child.
- Nora shows Mrs Linde her costume for the party.
- They discuss Dr Rank's illness. Mrs Linde warns Nora about her closeness with the doctor.
- Nora explains that Rank is not the source of the loan.

CONTEXT

The origins of the sexually transmitted diseases gonorrhoea and syphilis were hazy in this period. In fact, a child would not inherit syphilis, but could be infected if the mother had been infected before conceiving. If aware of this distinction, Ibsen may have chosen to ignore it in order to develop the parallels between Rank and Nora as children betrayed by their fathers and to make it clear that this is an illness that afflicts all levels of society.

As the curtain rises Nora is restless, listening out for visitors and checking the letter box for a note from Krogstad. The nurse arrives with Nora's fancy dress, which is torn. Nora asks after the children, and the nurse says they are missing her. This prompts Nora to ask if the nurse – who cared for her as a child – misses her own child, whom she gave up. Philosophically, the nurse says that she had no alternative but to leave her daughter, but has had two letters from her since.

Mrs Linde arrives and Nora shows her the dress, explaining that Helmer wants her to dance the tarantella at the party. Mrs Linde begins to repair the dress and asks about Dr Rank. She is a little shocked that Nora understands the nature of Rank's disease, congenital syphilis, and is also puzzled that Rank seemed to know who she was when they were introduced. Nora reveals that she has talked about her to Rank, as Helmer dislikes discussing her old friends. Mrs Linde is concerned at the apparent closeness between Nora and Dr Rank, and asks if the doctor is the source of the loan. Nora denies it, and is about to tell her more, when Helmer returns. She hustles Mrs Linde out of the room.

COMMENTARY

The sight of the Christmas tree stripped of presents indicates that time has passed and it is Christmas Day; the presence of Nora's cloak suggests she might want to go out. But as she speaks

– 'A thing like that *couldn't* happen' (p. 181) – she is virtually repeating what she said at the close of Act 1, implying that she has spent twenty-four hours in paralysing terror. The burnt-out candles reflect this mood. Nora is evidently contemplating leaving her children seriously enough to hint that she trusts the nurse with them.

Although the nurse features little in the play, this scene is of great importance. Firstly, it shows us a moment of genuine love in contrast to the complex game-playing and self-deception at the heart of the Helmers' marriage. Secondly, it brings into the play the wider world of female experience. The nurse's story is tragic, but her matter-of-fact tone about girls who 'got into trouble' (p. 182) and her touchingly low expectations (two letters in a period as long as Nora's own lifetime) remind us that such stories are common in the 'community' everyone has been glibly discussing. Finally, although the nurse has never enjoyed Nora's material advantages, both are equally powerless under the law: if there were a divorce, Helmer could take the children from her. The nurse is yet another figure in the hall of mirrors in which Nora finds herself trapped.

Nora's irritation with her fancy dress – 'I should like to tear it all to pieces' (p. 181) – reflects her earlier comment to Helmer that 'Everything seems so stupid and pointless' (Act 1, p. 178) and suggests that the dress is acquiring a **symbolic** significance for her. Helmer's choice of a Neapolitan fisher-girl's outfit may reflect his sense of social superiority to Nora; the dress is also a souvenir of the Italian holiday for which Nora has gone into debt. When Mrs Linde says that she would like to see her 'all dressed up' in it (p. 183), Ibsen employs the same word used to describe the Christmas tree. Nora is perhaps growing weary of 'dressing up' for Helmer as his social and sexual inferior, and of being 'dressed up' like a doll by him. We may see her as vulnerable to the same fate as the tree she bought earlier, now stripped of its finery and unwanted.

 CHECK THE BOOK

A. S. Byatt's novel *The Biographer's Tale* (2000) explores Ibsen's preoccupation with doubles and characters who mirror one another. In the section of the book called 'The third document' Byatt dramatises an encounter between Ibsen and his illegitimate son, Hans Jacob, who is sitting in Ibsen's special chair in the café, dressed in one of his father's own discarded suits, and quotes from several of Ibsen's plays which deal with the subject of heredity.

CHECK THE BOOK

Ibsen: A Dissenting View (1977) shows how Ibsen can still be misunderstood in exactly the same way as he was in the nineteenth century. Ronald Gray considers Nora's expectations 'unrealistic', but – just as in the 1870s – this is perceived as *Ibsen's* problem. The presence of the nurse is labelled a 'dramatic flaw' – she is not a factor in Nora's choice to leave, but a convenience to prevent our 'full recognition of how bleak and unrealistic [Nora's] decision is'. For more critical views see **Part Four**.

GLOSSARY

182 **Nanny** poorer women with illegitimate or dead babies would be employed to breastfeed the children of wealthy mothers (or perhaps in Nora's case, because the mother had died)

confirmed formally received into the Church. Nora mentions being confirmed on p. 228 (probably in her early teens for a Norwegian Protestant like Nora)

muff a woollen or fur tube to warm the hands

184 **delicate** an expression that covers any form of poor or weak health

PAGES 186–90

- Nora asks Helmer to give Krogstad a job and he resists.
- When she presses him, he sends Krogstad a note of dismissal.
- Helmer promises Nora that he can cope with any consequences.

Nora greets Helmer enthusiastically and starts pleading for 'something' (p. 187); he is indulgent until he realises she is raising the subject of Krogstad again. Nora mentions that Krogstad writes for the newspapers and may damage Helmer. He thinks she is comparing him to her father, who was vilified by the press and would have lost his job if Helmer had not helped him. Helmer smugly notes: 'Your father's reputation as an official was not above suspicion – mine is' (p. 188), adding that he would be a 'laughing-stock' at the bank if they realised he could be influenced by his wife.

He then tells Nora the most important reason to get rid of Krogstad: he calls Helmer by his Christian name! Nora finds this 'petty' and says so (p. 189). Peeved, Helmer orders the maid to post the letter of dismissal. Nora is terrified of the consequences but Helmer announces that he is 'man enough' to cope alone (p. 190). This leaves her even more afraid. Knowing the outcome will be more severe than anything Helmer imagines, she promises him that he will not have to do this. He patronisingly says that they will 'share it as man and wife' and dismisses her to practise her dance.

COMMENTARY

A clue is dropped so subtly in this episode that it is easy to miss: Nora's father would evidently have lost his job if Helmer had not been 'so kind and helpful' (p. 188). Is this a **euphemism** for a willingness to cover up underhand dealing? If so, Helmer may, even unconsciously, have seen Nora as his reward for silence. Ibsen's comedy is especially sharp in this episode; however, this is not comic relief for its own sake. Each outburst about Krogstad is prompted by a stimulus from Nora; their exchanges make it increasingly apparent that the couple are moving in opposite directions. Nora begins in her usual wheedling tone; but then her argument becomes logical as she questions his fear of seeming subject to her influence; finally, she uses overtly critical language about Helmer for the first time, calling him 'petty' (p. 189). She may even be laughing at him. The audience certainly will, as under her gaze his pomposity blooms like some great exotic flower until he blurts his childish 'There, little Miss Stubborn!' (p. 189).

While the action hitherto has shown Nora's relationship to the womanly ideal of her time, it now begins to explore the construction of masculinity. Helmer's pompous self-assurance about his 'courage and strength' (p. 190) is funny but suggests he is living out a stereotype rather than truly knowing himself. He is not 'strong' – he has previously collapsed from overwork; and he is not courageous enough to deal with the presence of a subordinate, Krogstad, who reminds him that the class divide between them was once much narrower.

CHECK THE FILM

Two film versions of *A Doll's House* appeared in 1973, one directed by Patrick Garland and starring Claire Bloom as Nora, Anthony Hopkins as Helmer and Denholm Elliott as Krogstad; the other directed by Joseph Losey and starring Jane Fonda as Nora, David Warner as Helmer and Edward Fox as Krogstad.

CHECK THE NET

For a full cast list of both 1973 films of *A Doll's House*, together with details on the 1992 televised film version, search the Internet Movie Database at **www.imdb.com**

GLOSSARY

189   **scribbler** a poor-quality journalist (Krogstad describes himself as one on p. 197)

PAGES 190–6

- Dr Rank arrives and tells Nora that he is dying.
- They flirt over her costume and she is on the verge of asking him for money.
- He confesses his love for her, and she realises that she cannot.

Dr Rank arrives and Nora tells him Helmer is busy. He reveals that one more test will inform him when he is likely to die. He considers Helmer too sensitive to witness his dying, and promises to send Nora a card with a black cross on it when the final stage of his disease begins. He complains of the injustice of hereditary illness and wonders if Mrs Linde has already replaced him as Nora's friend.

Nora shows him the silk stockings she will wear to the party and they banter suggestively. He says he would like to express his gratitude to her and she mentions 'a terribly great favour' (p. 194). Rank tells her that he would 'gladly give his life' for her; suddenly Nora cannot continue and reproves him for saying it. She now refuses to ask the favour. Rank wonders if he should leave, but she persuades him that they should remain friends. She explains that she loves to talk with him – there are 'people that one loves, and others that perhaps one would rather be with' (p. 196). The maid enters with Krogstad's card; Nora pretends a new dress has arrived and asks Rank to go and keep Helmer busy.

CHECK THE BOOK

Elizabeth Gaskell's novel *Ruth* (1853) challenges nineteenth-century attitudes to women in a story of an unmarried mother. However, although Ruth is seen as a brave, competent and much wronged figure, the novel ends with her death after she nurses the father of her child through typhus: only thus could she be seen as 'redeemed' from her initial sin.

COMMENTARY

For the first time in the play we see an adult encounter, refreshing after the relentless infantilising of Nora by Helmer and even Mrs Linde. The audience too are expected to think like adults. The presence of an invalid in literature of the period often indicated that a character like Nora, who had sinned in some way, was to get a chance to redeem herself through selflessly nursing him. Nora's selfish relief when Rank's bad news turns out to be about his illness indicates that the play will not indulge in such a sentimental cliché. Rank also crucially confirms our growing suspicion of Helmer.

We may until now have seen Nora's concern for him as fussy; Rank is the only person in the play with the same status and power as Helmer, yet he too is a member of the 'Torvald Helmer Protection Society' and wishes to keep his 'sensitive' nature from unpleasant truths (p. 191).

This scene is an example of subtext: unspoken ideas and emotions pulsing beneath commonplace words and actions. Rank and Nora speak in a code that reveals both themselves and their world. First, it makes clear that Nora understands Rank's situation, and he knows it. It also stresses that this is knowledge forbidden to her sex and class; when Nora mentions 'asparagus and *foie gras*' (p. 192) she parrots the kind of lie with which an enquiring woman might be fobbed off; her tag question to Rank – 'isn't that it?' – challenges him to repeat such a lie with a straight face. When he counters it with 'truffles' he indicates that he approves of her worldly knowledge (Helmer, one imagines, would prefer women to be innocent and ignorant). Nora's riposte about 'oysters' – reputedly an aphrodisiac – shows her awareness that Rank's father had syphilis; 'What a shame that all those nice things should attack the bones' brings Rank back to his original complaint that his own spine is paying the price, despite never having had 'the least enjoyment' (p. 192). This develops the theme of heredity introduced by Helmer's strictures on Nora's father.

Rank's role has previously been that of the stock nineteenth-century character the *raisonneur*, the intelligent bystander who helps the audience interpret the action. Suddenly he becomes not only a character with his own story, but another mirror of Nora. Both are victims of corrupt parents. Her reply, however, alters the direction of this exchange. 'Yes, that's the saddest part of all' (p. 192) is a truism, but Rank's response suggests that Nora's expression has changed. He searches her face hoping, perhaps, for confirmation that she means 'the saddest part is that therefore we cannot be lovers'. Their hasty retreat into laughter, and her rapid mention of 'Torvald', implies mutual awareness of skirting a dangerous corner. Rank's appeal for pity – 'those who go away are quickly forgotten' (p. 192) – unwittingly plunges Nora back into contemplating the departure on her mind since her conversation with the nurse. She

> **CONTEXT**
>
> Anton Chekhov wrote this famous description of the role of subtext in **naturalistic** drama: 'It is necessary that on the stage everything should be as complex and as simple as in life. People are having dinner, and while they're having it, their future happiness may be decided or their lives may be about to be shattered' (quoted in J. L. Styan's *The Dark Comedy*, 1962, second edition 1968, p. 75).

obviously feels that she can still ask Rank for the money, perhaps because she has in her own mind a clear definition of real love: Helmer 'wouldn't hesitate for a moment to give his life for me' (p. 194). But by abandoning **subtext** and speaking plainly, she has now put love, not sex, back on the agenda and Rank falls gratefully on the opportunity to do the same.

This, rather than Krogstad's threats, is the most intense moment of crisis for Nora. It shows clearly Ibsen's method of transcending a stock situation. The heroine of a **well-made play** might face the choice between unwanted sexual attentions or financial ruin, and the audience could respond sentimentally to her 'fall' or her piety. The audience here may be in **suspense**, wondering if Nora will compromise herself. It is for the actress to choose exactly how she will show Nora reach her decision not to ask the 'favour', but it is a moment of moral growth, not melodrama. Does her *'slight start'* (p. 194) indicate a first shocked realisation? Or has she begun to sense what Rank is going to say earlier in the scene? Does she at some point become aware that she is attempting to manipulate her friend for money, as she has habitually manipulated her husband?

Nora's request for the lamp is a definite change of gear and an example of Ibsen's subtle use of staging. She exploits the new lighting **symbolically**; by saying to Rank, 'Aren't you ashamed of yourself, now that the lamp's come in?' (p. 195), she closes the subject definitively, implying that his declaration belongs to the dark rather than the light of goodness. Because the lamp is real, however, the tone is kept graciously at the level of banter, not reproof. This is a woman who is beginning to make decisions for herself. The sequence sets a moral standard by which we will now judge Helmer and his response to Krogstad's threat. The lamp also reminds us that the day is wearing on, and there is little time left.

See **Text 1** of **Extended commentaries** for further discussion of part of this section.

CONTEXT

St Lucy's Day, the old winter solstice, is a festival of light in Scandinavia. A young woman wearing a crown of lighted candles brings food to the door of each house in her village, and fires are lit to symbolise the breaking of the power of winter. Nora taps into this symbolism as a bringer of light in the darkness.

? QUESTION

How does Ibsen use light and darkness in the play?

GLOSSARY

192	*foie gras* goose liver pâté, very expensive
196	*card* visitors handed a calling card to the maid, who would bring it to her employer to be told whether to admit the caller
	back stairs conventionally the entrance for servants. Krogstad's furtive use of them may surprise the maid

PAGES 196–206

- Krogstad enters and informs Nora that the price of his silence is a better job at the bank. He drops a letter in the box explaining this to Helmer.
- Nora tells Mrs Linde, who offers to intercede with her former admirer Krogstad.
- Nora tries to distract Helmer from the letter by rehearsing her dance for the party.

As the maid goes to usher in Krogstad, Nora bolts the door to Helmer's study. Krogstad at first professes to assume that Nora must have told her husband what she has done; when she says that Helmer does not know, he tells her that he will make nothing public for the present because 'it can just be arranged between us three' (p. 198). He says he has no intention of giving her the IOU and has brought a letter to Helmer spelling out the situation. He goes on to ask if she has any idea of running away or committing suicide. She is amazed that he has guessed this, and he tells her that he too had contemplated killing himself, but lacked the courage – as she does. Nora offers him more money, but he explains that what he wants is a better job. Nora threatens to kill herself, but he points out that her reputation would still be entirely in his hands. Krogstad leaves, and after a moment his letter drops into the box.

Mrs Linde returns with the mended dress, and in a panic Nora tells her everything. Afraid that she might go mad, Nora claims full responsibility for her action, alluding to a mysterious 'miracle' that

CHECK THE BOOK

Krogstad's line 'People don't do such things' (p. 200) was repeated in 1890 in *Hedda Gabler*. The last line of the play, it is a comment on the suicide of the central character, who shoots herself rather than be in the power of a man with damaging information about her.

CONTEXT

The tarantella was originally a folk dance but was developed by a Madame Michau in the 1840s for more polite circles. It involves gallops, slides and twirls and is very fast-paced – Nora clearly has talent to attempt a solo.

must be prevented (p. 201). Mrs Linde offers to talk to Krogstad, who once 'would gladly have done anything' for her (p. 202). Suddenly Helmer bangs on his door, and Mrs Linde hurries off to visit Krogstad. Nora unlocks the door and Helmer enters with Dr Rank; Nora asks her husband to spend the evening helping her rehearse the tarantella. Just as he is about to head into the hall to see if any letters have arrived, she begins to dance, more and more wildly; she is still dancing when Mrs Linde returns. Helmer criticises Nora for forgetting 'everything I taught you' (p. 204) and promises to spend all evening and the following day coaching her, although he warns her that once she has danced at tomorrow night's party she will not 'have her own way' (p. 205).

As dinner is announced Nora calls for champagne and macaroons. Mrs Linde quietly tells her that she could not find Krogstad but has left him a note. Nora is now convinced that a 'miracle' will occur – and, alone on the stage, makes it clear that she intends to kill herself after the party, which gives her 'thirty-one hours to live' (p. 206).

CHECK THE NET

You can find out how to dance the tarantella and see some pictures of fisher-girls in traditional costume at **www. virtualitalia.com/ articles** – look under 'other features'.

COMMENTARY

Krogstad's entrance via the back stairs shows a new bravado; Ibsen marks this with costume. In Act 1, on legitimate business with Helmer, Krogstad waited deferentially while the maid took his coat. Here he is in outdoor clothes, suggesting that he has pushed past her. His boots and fur cap indicate that it is freezing outside, reminding the audience of the darkness and cold – both real and **metaphorical** – into which Nora will step at the end of the play.

Krogstad's language is now less respectful, even presumptuous – but, interestingly, this disrespect is largely directed towards 'our worthy Torvald Helmer' (p. 197), who 'daren't so much as murmur' (p. 199). Krogstad is the only person who expresses such outright contempt, and its straightforwardness contrasts with the complexity of his attitude to Nora. His sense that Nora may contemplate suicide suggests that his insistence on their similarity is more than a desire to rub Nora's nose in her criminal status. He seems actively '*relieved*' that she has renounced suicide (p. 198). While the previous act showed Krogstad to be more than a stage **villain**, he now offers an almost **metatheatrical** comment on the crudity of **stock characters**. His brisk deflation of Nora's image of heroic suicide with a graphic description of her corpse – 'ugly, hairless, unrecognizable' (p. 200) – would have shocked a nineteenth-century audience used to idealist images of noble women.

Krogstad's exit is a piece of carefully crafted **suspense**. The audience is briefly teased with the possibility that he may not leave the letter. Then it arrives, to provide a visual reminder of Nora's danger. This device is commonplace, but here it develops our awareness of the boundaries of the 'house'; the space is not just a handy setting for the action but reflects Nora's physical and spiritual confinement. Krogstad's noisy footsteps – nobody else walks audibly – are not followed by the sound of the front door closing. It is, in a sense, left 'open' until Helmer forcefully locks it in the next act. However, the wildness of Nora's tarantella shows her like an animal in a trap, caught between two men who love her but fail her. Rank's **aside** to Helmer – 'There isn't anything …? I mean, she's not expecting …?' (p. 205) – shows even this loving friend does not understand her. The passion of the music and the energy of her movement underline that the action is moving towards the **strong curtain** with which the **well-made play** typically closes its penultimate act.

See **Text 2** of **Extended commentaries** for further discussion of part of this section.

CHECK THE BOOK

Jerome K. Jerome's *Stage-Land* (1889) contains an amusing summary of the stock characters to be found in popular drama, including the heroine, the serving girl and the villain, of whom he writes: 'The stage villain is superior to the villain of real life. The villain of real life is actuated by mere sordid and selfish motives. The stage villain does villainy, not for any personal advantage to himself, but merely from the love of the thing as an art. Villainy is to him its own reward; he revels in it.'

QUESTION

Imagine that you are one of the original audience watching the play at the point when the curtain comes down at the end of the second act. How, in terms of your nineteenth-century perspective, do you think the story will end, and why?

GLOSSARY

204   *particoloured* made of patches of brightly coloured material; associated with the theatrical

205   expecting a euphemism for 'pregnant'

ACT 3

PAGES 207–15

- Krogstad comes to see Mrs Linde at the Helmers' and they reach a new understanding.
- Krogstad wishes to take back his letter but Mrs Linde urges him not to.
- Helmer brings Nora home after her dance.
- Helmer tries to make love to Nora but they are interrupted.

CHECK THE BOOK

Lesley Ferris's *Acting Women: Images of Women in Theatre* (1990) is a wide-ranging study of female performance across history, and the chapter entitled 'The Wilful Woman' is particularly useful in considering *A Doll's House*.

As the curtain rises Mrs Linde is waiting anxiously for someone, who proves to be Krogstad. They discuss their past: she ended their relationship to marry a wealthier man and this still rankles, although she feels she had no choice but to support her mother and brothers. Krogstad reproaches her for taking his former job at the bank; she refuses to give it up, but gently suggests they 'join forces' (p. 209), saying she came to town specifically to find him. She wants someone to 'work for' (p. 209). Krogstad is sceptical but Mrs Linde wins him round; both think he can be 'a different man' (p. 210) with her support. They hear the sounds of the tarantella from the party above and he wishes he could undo the blackmail. He resolves to do what Mrs Linde had summoned him to ask – to reclaim his letter unread from Helmer. However, Mrs Linde now feels that there must be 'complete understanding' (p. 211) between Nora and Helmer. Krogstad leaves when Mrs Linde hears that the dance is over.

Nora and Helmer return and he explains he insisted on leaving early in order not to undermine the effect of her dance. Mrs Linde snatches a moment with Nora to tell her that she has 'nothing to fear from Krogstad' (p. 213) but that the letter will inform Helmer of the truth if she does not confess herself. Helmer gives Mrs Linde a short lecture on the merits of embroidery rather than knitting and she leaves. Relieved to be alone with his wife, Helmer tells her that he likes to pretend they are newly-weds. He begins to make romantic advances, when there is a knock on the door.

COMMENTARY

The opening of this act teases the audience. Because the tension has been escalating, they expect it to begin, like the previous one, with Nora and her mounting panic. Instead the curtain rises on Mrs Linde. For a brief moment, Ibsen seems to indulge the desire for tense emotion as she watches anxiously for Krogstad; but on his arrival the audience must accept that they are going to be watching two people quietly discussing their own concerns. This increases the **suspense** but also acts as a salutary reminder that everyone has a story of their own: the **villain** and the **confidante** – not a combination generally seen in plays using **stock characters** – are stepping out of their dramatic functions to take the stage in their own right.

The entrance of Nora and Helmer shows Ibsen's keen sense of visual spectacle. Their appearance contrasts sharply with Mrs Linde; both are in fancy dress that befits the way both 'perform' what society expects of their gender. His cloak over ordinary evening clothes suggests that he wants to give the impression of being above anything so childish as 'dressing up' – although, of course, this choice reflects a fantasy about himself as much as any fancy costume could. He sees the costume he has chosen for Nora as that of a '*capricious* little Capri girl' (p. 213) – a changeable child from an alien culture, not part of the 'real' world of money, morality and decision-making. The way he takes Nora's shawl off to display her for Mrs Linde's admiration is a visual sign of Nora's developing problems: in Act 1 she spoke proudly of saving money by buying cheap dresses; here, literally dressed by Helmer, she is losing even that small independence.

We have just heard Mrs Linde's optimistic assumption that the truth will somehow help their marriage. However, her attempt to tell Nora is juxtaposed with an episode which suggests that Helmer and reality are strangers: his hilarious demonstration of how to embroider and knit. This offers a physically adept actor a piece of **stage business** as interesting as Nora's tarantella; while she performed a sexualised image of femininity, this large man in his evening suit demonstrates how to be a domestic goddess, a **drag act**

 CHECK THE BOOK

In Charlotte Brontë's *Jane Eyre* (1847) Jane feels compromised by her future husband's insistence on choosing clothes for her, a process she considers is making him behave like a sultan to his slave: 'he fixed on a rich silk of the most brilliant amethyst dye, and a superb pink satin. I told him in a new series of whispers, that he might as well buy me a gold gown and a silver bonnet at once' (Chapter 24).

in miniature that he would never have attempted if not decidedly tipsy. Mrs Linde's face as he bustles her out will be an interesting contrast to her speech as polite employee, calling him 'Mr Helmer' (p. 214).

While the actors are given considerable freedom as to how they play Helmer's advances and Nora's resistance, Helmer should probably not seem too much of a predator here. Drunkenness seems unfamiliar to him and he acts like an adolescent, his sexual fantasies of the bride-Nora so vivid that he is oblivious to the **irony** in remarks like 'I know that you're always thinking of me' (p. 215). The *real* Nora, exhausted and anxious, is invisible to him.

See **Text 3** of **Extended commentaries** for further discussion of part of this section.

> **GLOSSARY**
>
> 211   *domino* a cloak with a hood, a compromise between fancy dress and plain evening wear
>
> 213   *capricious* wilful and changeable

PAGES 216–22

CHECK THE NET

The Ibsen Society of America was founded in 1978; it offers a range of articles and information on Ibsen at **www. ibsensociety.liu. edu**

- Dr Rank calls. Nora asks about his last test and he lets her know that his death is certain. He leaves after a final goodbye.
- Helmer finds Rank's cards with the black cross. He still presses Nora to make love, but she tells him to read his letters, intending to kill herself.
- Helmer discovers Krogstad's letter and erupts in a rage.

Helmer answers the door; it is Dr Rank. Helmer greets him with an insincerity bordering on sarcasm and they recall the champagne at the party. Rank speaks of his 'good day's work' (p. 216) and Nora realises that he has performed his final test. He tells her the result is certain. Nora and Rank discuss their costumes for the next party and he says he will wear 'the Invisible Hat' (p. 217), mystifying Helmer. Rank asks for a cigar; Nora lights it for him and they wish each other goodbye.

Helmer decides to empty the letter box, complaining that someone has tried to force the lock. He finds two cards from Dr Rank marked with a black cross. Nora explains that this signifies Rank's impending death and Helmer reflects that now they will be alone more often. He resumes his attempt to make love; Nora tells him to read his letters. When this does not stop him she reminds him that it would hardly be fitting after Rank's news, and he agrees that they should sleep apart.

Helmer takes the letters into his study, and Nora prepares herself to leave, clearly intending suicide. Helmer suddenly flings open his door and demands to know the meaning of Krogstad's letter. He tells her she has ruined his life and that their future together can be nothing but a sham.

COMMENTARY

A moment ago it seemed inevitable that Helmer's insistence would trigger the final confrontation. Instead the audience is teased with another postponement which proves to be one of the most extraordinary sequences in the play. Rank's bland reply to Helmer's lack of courtesy, 'I thought I heard you talking' (p. 216), makes it painfully clear he has heard Helmer's advances and Nora's rejection of them. In this dark and very modern **comedy** of embarrassment, Nora's remarks about champagne and high spirits draw Rank into an alliance against Helmer. Their private code is still outwardly frivolous; but this time it is charged with intense sadness and repeatedly punctuated by silly remarks from an uncomprehending Helmer, the butt trapped between them in a reverse image of the Act 2 trio where the men watched the tarantella. Nora's gesture of lighting the cigar takes on a ritual quality picked up by Rank with his comment 'thank you for the light' (p. 218). It simultaneously connotes truth, virtue and the idea that she 'lights up' his life; the word can also be translated as 'fire' with all its overtones of warmth and passion: these will in any case be present through the sight of the flame she carries.

CONTEXT

In 1959 Cliff Richard's version of Lionel Bart's 'Living Doll' (Bart won an Ivor Novello Award for this song) was number one for six weeks. The lyrics, which talk about imprisoning the 'doll' so that nobody can entice her away, express the spirit of Helmer, who sees Rank's death as a chance to be alone with his wife.

Helmer's desire to 'risk everything' (p. 219) for his wife is a drunken boast, but it is a crucial moment for Nora, and her **body language** and expression as she insists that he read his letters are important. His speech provides confirmation that she can expect a 'miracle' of noble sacrifice from Helmer, and yet in this scene she has seemed close to despising him. The fragmented rhythm of her **soliloquy** on suicide (p. 220) – carefully reflected in this translation – and her instinctive choice of Helmer's garment to wrap around her suggest real and painful feelings; but the phrases themselves are **clichés** and the shawl over her head suggests a heroine of **melodrama**. It is as if she is forcing herself against all reason to take Helmer's heroics at face value because she cannot imagine a bearable alternative – even if it means she must act her correspondingly noble part to a fatal end.

CHECK THE FILM

In Patrick Garland's 1973 film of *A Doll's House* Helmer (played by Anthony Hopkins) strikes Claire Bloom's Nora when he has read the letter. The bruise is visible for the rest of the film.

As Helmer emerges from his study, the stage picture mirrors the beginning of Act 1 when he popped out to reprove his 'little featherbrain' (p. 148). One of the cruellest **ironies** of the scene is his repetition of a new and more insulting description for Nora: 'shiftless' (p. 221). Literally meaning 'without resources' and carrying connotations of idleness, it nevertheless denotes the flighty child-wife he has wanted Nora to be. By locking the door and proclaiming, 'Here you shall stay until you've explained yourself' (p. 220), he underlines his part in confining her to the 'doll's house'.

Equally ironic is Helmer's failure to realise that Nora intends to take responsibility for her action and carry out her suicide, while his own heroics of a few minutes ago are only 'fine phrases' (p. 221). The only future he can imagine is one which will be *all* 'acting', where Nora will continue the role of loving wife to save his reputation. By allowing Helmer explicitly to use the word 'melodrama' (p. 220) for the first time in the play, Ibsen seems to be forcing his nineteenth-century audience to realise that the simplistic moral codes of the previous generation of playwrights are being tested to destruction. Nora and Helmer themselves have frequently resorted to the language of melodrama. Indeed, it is difficult for them to find a vocabulary in which to express their deepest feelings which does not rely on sexual stereotypes. This is the real weakness of their relationship – although it has also, perhaps, kept them together.

GLOSSARY

217	mascot a lucky charm, personal to the owner
	Havanas Cuban cigars, the most expensive kind
218	hairpin in this period, a simple piece of bent wire; women's elaborate hairstyles required a large number of these

CHECK THE FILM

An adaptation of *A Doll's House* was shown by the BBC in 1992. The impressive cast for this televised film included Juliet Stevenson as Nora, Trevor Eve as Helmer and David Calder as Krogstad, and was directed by David Thacker.

PAGES 222–32

- A letter arrives from Krogstad returning the document with the forged signature.
- Helmer rejoices that he is saved, but ignores his wife.
- He goes on to forgive her at great length, while she changes her clothes.
- Nora emerges in everyday dress and says that she is leaving him.

There is a ring at the front door; a letter arrives for Nora, which Helmer snatches to read himself. It is from Krogstad, returning Nora's note of hand. Helmer gives a cry of joy: 'I'm saved!' (p. 222), leaving Nora to enquire, 'And I?' Happily burning the documents, Helmer announces that he has forgiven her. He goes on to tell her how he loves her helplessness and how, in time, she will come to understand how great is his forgiveness. Nora goes drearily out to take off her fancy dress as he expands on his theme. She returns in '*everyday things*' (p. 224), and tells him that they must talk.

Helmer becomes increasingly puzzled as she explains that she has been 'wronged' (p. 225) by both her father and him, treated as a plaything and encouraged to treat her children in the same way. Helmer decides it is now 'lesson-time' (p. 226); but, as she points out, he does not have the ability to educate her. She must do it herself, so she is going to leave him. He appeals to her 'sacred duties' (p. 227) as a wife and mother; she replies that her first duty is to herself. He invokes both religion and conscience, but she claims that she cannot accept what she has been taught any longer: she must find out for herself 'which is right – the world or I' (p. 229).

Helmer finally realises that 'You don't love me any more' (p. 229). Nora explains that she changed this evening: she thought the man she loved would step forward and take the blame for the forgery, and she fully intended to commit suicide to prevent such a sacrifice. Helmer's refusal even to consider sacrificing his own *'honour'* (p. 230), the selfishness of his relief at being 'saved' (p. 222) and his inability to realise that the marriage is now irrevocably changed have made him a 'stranger' (p. 232). He pleads with her to wait, to live as his sister, at least to return some day. But Nora can promise nothing. She does not know what will happen to her, but she says that 'the greatest miracle of all' would have to happen before they could live together – 'Both of us would have to be so changed that … our life together could be a real marriage' (p. 232). As Helmer ponders this she leaves, and the play closes with the slamming of the front door.

COMMENTARY

Ibsen's stagecraft is striking here. While every **well-made play** involves a compromising document – a letter, a note, a will – the IOU here gathers more sinister significance by *ceasing* to be a threat; its return does not form the centre of a happy **tableau** demonstrating the result of Krogstad's change of heart. Instead we see the half-dressed and obviously puzzled maid, expected to work in the middle of the night but stopped by Helmer from doing her job; the silent Nora humiliated in front of the servant; and Helmer grabbing what is, after all, the property of his wife.

Krogstad has written to Nora – the person he sees as his mirror – rather than his despised employer. Not only does Helmer interpret the letter as *his* salvation rather than Nora's, he has no interest in Krogstad's change of heart – even though this event has taken place in his own living room. The whole episode, for Helmer, proves that people behave according to stereotype. Unconsciously he is denying the very possibility of individual change by burning the letter that describes it, and he feels able to forgive his 'songbird' as a stereotypical hero should. (Though one might ask what, exactly,

CHECK THE POEM

Thomas Hardy's late poem 'She Did Not Turn' shows a man watching his wife passing the gate 'foot-faint with averted head' instead of coming into the house.

CONTEXT

The critic Clement Scott had little sympathy for Nora's final departure: 'It would be a miracle if [Helmer] could ever live again with so unnatural a creature' (*Theatre*, July 1889).

he is forgiving: her action has not harmed him and its motive was to do him good.)

Helmer's **rhetoric** allows the actress time to take 'off my fancy-dress' (p. 223). But it also gives the audience a challenging space to consider what they want to see next. Many of Ibsen's first audience would have expected a meek entrance in nightwear by a wife prepared to confine herself still more closely in the home; twenty-first-century audiences, perhaps, might hope that the very extravagance of Helmer's speech will alert Nora to the impossibility of doing so.

The 'reckoning' at the table is structured with great care; points are raised and discussed almost as if we are in the courtroom where Helmer once worked, and the arguments move from the house itself to the wider world into which Nora will emerge. It begins with Nora's domestic unhappiness – which Helmer hopes to change by changing *her* with an 'education' he can administer. Then it moves to the political: Helmer appeals to all aspects of male **hegemony**: public opinion, **patriarchy**, the Church, the law. Nora counters these with the right of the individual not to change these but to interrogate them. Then – after one last attempt by Helmer at heroic generalisation about what men do – the conversation returns to the personal, but this time the subject is Helmer himself. Still unable to grasp that he needs to change as much as Nora, he tries to suggest what 'we' might do before the loss of her love renders his situation tragically specific.

This slow but inexorable dismantling of the relationship makes a solid frame for what must be read as a scene of real emotional intensity in which both characters are in pain. Nora and Helmer have both done their best within their limited understanding of love, and while Nora wants to redefine it, she is not trying to punish the man who has 'wronged' her (p. 225); she even accepts her share of responsibility for the 'tricks' (p. 226). But she has already taken off the fancy dress while Helmer is still 'dressed up'. It will be harder for him to abandon his illusions, simply because society will be on his side – as Nora points out, he is 'legally freed from all his obligations to her' (p. 231).

 QUESTION

Ibsen makes use of the well-made play structure with moments of crisis, **strong curtains** and a powerful **denouement**. As Nora is his central character, these are all from her point of view. If you wrote a **scenario** for an alternative version of *A Doll's House* focusing on Mrs Linde or Krogstad, what scenes, endings and moments of crisis might be needed?

CHECK THE POEM

Robert Browning (1812–89) wrote many **dramatic monologues**, including 'The Last Ride Together', spoken by a man whose mistress is leaving him, who persuades her to take one final ride with him. In reflecting 'Who knows but the world may end tonight?' he echoes Helmer's hope of a miracle.

CHECK THE NET

You can read this poem by Browning online at **www.online-literature.com**

As the scene moves to its close, Helmer is more and more physically isolated in the doll's house as Nora gathers her possessions together to leave. Finally it is 'Empty!' and all he has left is the idea of a 'miracle' (p. 232). In Ibsen's first draft Helmer cried, 'I believe in them.' In the final draft he cries, '*I'll* believe in them' (Egil Törnqvist, *A Doll's House*, 1995, pp. 39–40, my italics). What he has to believe in is the possibility that both he and Nora can become individuals capable of moral choice. Ibsen's **ambiguous** wording does not suggest optimism. However, Helmer is alone, quietly talking to himself as Nora did at the start of the play, when her journey began. At this early point it suggested loneliness, as it does with Helmer now. But it was only alone that Nora was able to set out on her journey at the start of the play.

EXTENDED COMMENTARIES

TEXT 1 – ACT 2, PAGE 193

From 'Now be nice, Dr Rank' to 'Take that!'

At this point in the play Dr Rank has, perhaps, been trying to decide whether or not Nora is in love with him and has expressed a little jealousy of Mrs Linde as his possible replacement in Nora's affections. He has inadvertently raised the topic of absence, and Nora is at this point contemplating her own – either by leaving or by suicide. Nora's overtly flirtatious behaviour with the stockings she will wear at the party shocked Ibsen's rival and contemporary August Strindberg (1849–1912), who wrote: 'Nora offers herself for sale – to be paid for in cash' (quoted in *Ibsen's Lively Art: A Performance Study of the Major Plays* by Frederick J. Marker and Lise-Lone Marker, 1989, p. 87). However, the scene is more complex than this, and it is undoubtedly a mistake to see Nora's behaviour as a crude offer to sleep with Rank. It is partly an attempt to cheer herself up by reverting to their self-consciously comic performance of a few moments ago. It also shows her recognition that the dream of a love affair is important to Rank; by continuing to use this rather dangerously allusive language she is able to please him.

Nevertheless, Nora is certainly paving the way for her request for money. When she says, 'you'll see how beautifully I shall dance, and you can tell yourself that it's all for you', she is echoing her promise to 'dance on a moonbeam' in return for favours from Helmer (Act 2, p. 187). Repeated remarks like 'Come and sit here' and 'Look here' indicate that Nora is trying to bring Rank physically near her. His ability to identify the stockings as silk may well depend upon his touching them, offering the actors a moment of sensual closeness. The developing darkness Nora mentions has created an atmosphere of intimacy – people tend to speak quietly in the dark – and the frankness with which the doctor speaks of his impending death seems to be opening up the possibility of love between them. However, the double entendres are becoming cruder: 'you may see the rest, too' is a shocking remark for a respectable wife to make in a period when even to mention underwear would be considered startling. **Paradoxically**, the new crudity means an element of self-censorship has entered the conversation. Nora banters with Rank as if she is already his mistress, but the topic of love is excluded. Rank's own willingness to join the game with 'I can't possibly give you an opinion on that' (implying 'unless you let me see your legs') suggests that he too has decided to use the language of impropriety to postpone the discourse of love.

The stockings are a vital **prop** in this scene. Fragile and easily damaged, they provide a visual image of this whole encounter. Their association with the fisher-girl's outfit reminds us of the Italian holiday – and hence the debt – and of Helmer himself. They suggest both his inability to deal with unmitigated reality – surely a 'Neopolitan fisher-girl' (Act 2, p. 183) would not be able to afford flesh-coloured silk stockings? – and his sexual possessiveness in choosing Nora's most intimate garments. Nora may strike Rank with a stocking, but it is impossible to land a blow with a piece of silk: the effect is more like a kiss. The actors can stress the risqué aspect of this situation, and use it to create camaraderie between Nora and Rank. But they may prefer to make it a moment of tenderness. (In Ingmar Bergman's 1989 production, Nora gently covered Rank's eyes with the stocking as if blindfolding him before a death sentence was carried out.)

CHECK THE BOOK
Playwrights on Playwriting (1988), edited by Toby Cole, contains Ibsen's **scenario** for *A Doll's House*, which suggests the silk stockings are a late addition to the story.

CHECK THE BOOK
Eva Le Gallienne (1899–1991), a pioneer of women's theatre, staged her own productions of Ibsen in America in the 1920s, 1930s and 1940s, a period when he was considered 'box office poison'; she was a notable Nora, but her own translation of the play (1951) omits the silk stockings sequence, of which she disapproved.

CONTEXT

The spider originally called a tarantula was a wolf spider in southern Italy, discovered in the region around the seaport Taranto, and named *Lycosa tarantula*. This spider's bite was once thought to cause a fatal illness called tarantism.

CONTEXT

The word 'hysteria' derives from the Greek word for 'womb', and was originally thought to occur when the womb slipped upwards into the mouth. Female hysteria was a common medical diagnosis during the Victorian era for women who exhibited a wide array of symptoms including faintness, nervousness, insomnia, shortness of breath, irritability, loss of appetite – and a tendency to cause trouble.

TEXT 2 – ACT 2, PAGE 204

From 'Now play for me' to 'There! You see.'

Krogstad's letter exposing Nora is in the letter box. She has no escape now, but is determined to postpone the crisis for one last night. As Helmer insists on reading his letters she demands that he help her rehearse her dance. Ibsen never wrote a line of dialogue until he had composed a **scenario** describing what happened in every scene in minute detail. Nora's dance was not planned at this stage but added as the full draft developed. Ibsen first imagined an oriental dance to Anitra's music from Edvard Grieg's *Peer Gynt Suite*, with its erotic, slave-girl overtones, but opted for the less languorous and more energetic tarantella.

Although it is perfectly credible that Nora and Helmer might entertain the company with a dance they encountered on their Italian holiday, its significance here is complex. Ibsen's contemporaries were probably aware of the tarantella's origins: its name is derived from *tarantula*. The bite of this spider was thought to cause dance-like convulsions. But while these movements were the symptom of the disease, its only cure was believed to be to dance and sweat the poison out of the system. Nora is performing a kind of dance of death, expressing her thoughts of suicide and the fact that, as one of the 'lying mothers' that Helmer has been condemning, she is 'poisoning [her] own children with lies and deceit' (Act 1, p. 179). As the afflicted hoped that they could dance their way to a miraculous recovery, so too she expects a 'miracle' from Helmer, although it is one she will not allow to happen. When she responds to Mrs Linde's conventional praise that she is 'dancing as if your life depended on it!' with 'it does', she is speaking the truth as she sees it.

The wildness of Nora's dancing has been seen as a portrayal of female hysteria or as melodrama (Elizabeth Robins and Eleonora Duse, two notable early Noras, felt it beneath their dignity). Ibsen's direction that Nora's hair should fall '*over her shoulders*' refers to the **melodramatic** convention that unbound hair implies impending madness. However, while such exaggerated performance and images certainly occur in melodrama, the implication here seems to be that only an extreme theatricality can articulate Nora's true feelings. Helmer has repeatedly refused to have any kind of rational discussion on the subject of Krogstad; Rank has substituted emotion for practical help. Even at this moment, Nora is for both of them the object of a sexualised gaze, a dancing doll. They take turns at the piano: Rank's request to 'play for her' suggests he is taking Helmer's place in the only way available to him. As they discuss her, however, it is Mrs Linde Nora chooses to address; her line 'this is fun' can be translated more literally as '*watch* the fun' – she believes, perhaps, that only another woman can interpret what she sees as an expression of pain, rather than childishness or pregnancy (her excited state prompts Dr Rank's idiotic question on p. 205: 'she's not expecting …?').

The dance may be a diversion and it may be undisciplined, but it is also Nora's own dance; it runs counter to Helmer's shouted instructions and the rhythm he tries to conduct: Nora may even use the tambourine to assert a beat of her own. It is performed not to the neighbours to whom Helmer wants to show off his wife, but to the people to whom she wishes to communicate her feelings; and it is performed in clothing selected by her: the dress and shawl of the wife and mother she is, not that of a 'fisher-girl' from a class to which Helmer feels superior.

TEXT 3 – ACT 3, PAGES 207–11

From 'Well, Nils, let us have a talk' to 'the most marvellous thing that's ever happened to me'.

This is the culmination of all the scenes in which Nora has been faced with 'mirrors' of herself. Here two characters who share aspects of her experience and situation confront not Nora but each other. In doing so Mrs Linde and Krogstad foreshadow the final discussion between Helmer and Nora at the end of the play, even in their position on the stage, and the scene can be usefully read alongside this final episode.

CHECK THE FILM

Joseph Losey's 1973 film of *A Doll's House*, freely adapted in places, shows Jane Fonda as Nora dancing the tarantella twice: in her home, where she performs a kind of cancan that Helmer describes as a 'wanton display'; and again in costume at the party upstairs.

QUESTION

Examine Ibsen's use of characters as mirrors or doubles. How does this help the audience to consider the relationship between Nora and Helmer?

QUESTION

The dedication page of one of Ibsen's books contains the following statement: 'Writing means summoning oneself to court and playing the judge's part' (quoted in Harold Clurman, *Ibsen*, 1977, p. 24). Do you think this is what Ibsen does as writer of *A Doll's House*?

While we have seen Mrs Linde's independence as a possible model for Nora, the economic gap between them has made them seem very different. However, it is now plain that they share a similar experience: Helmer provided Nora's father with vital 'help' and won himself a wife; Mrs Linde made a conscious decision to take a husband who would provide for her family. Although Nora, passively passed from father to husband, has had better luck than the woman who mistakenly chose a wastrel, they share an experience of commodification, effectively sold to help their families. Both have lived in a doll's house; but only Mrs Linde has reached the understanding that Nora will acquire by the end of this act, and only Mrs Linde knows what life is like as someone who now refuses to be commodified. Meanwhile Krogstad, who has repeatedly insisted on his likeness to Nora as a fellow forger, now mirrors her in a more poignant way: he describes life with a ruined reputation – the fate he has wished on Nora. When he realises he has a chance to recover, he also wishes a similar redemption for her.

The characters are anchored at the table for most of this episode, which places them on an equal footing. Previously the space has tended to underline differences in the power of the sexes: Nora has moved around both Helmer and Rank, embracing, dancing and playing on their physical closeness. This neutral arrangement foreshadows their sober settling of accounts. Yet this is also a love scene, of a sort – with a woman as the active party. Mrs Linde has chosen the setting, by coming to town to find Krogstad; she has defined the nature of the relationship she wants: someone to 'work for' (p. 209), children 'to be a mother to' (p. 210). More significantly, she has defined its language and its moral basis. She is clear that her offer to care for him is not the **rhetoric** of 'a woman's exaggerated sense of nobility' (like that of Nora); rather, she has all the information about Krogstad's past but she assumes that love has the power to motivate change – to the point of transforming him into 'a different man' (p. 210). Picking up Krogstad's image of 'a shipwrecked man clinging to a spar', she offers a very unidealistic image of their future life together as 'Two on one spar' (p. 209). But it is enough for Krogstad to describe it, as he goes out by the front door, as 'the most marvellous thing that's ever happened to me' (p. 211). Nora will, in the same place on the stage, speak of 'the greatest miracle of all' (p. 232) – by which she means a genuine marriage of equals. Krogstad's line ensures that we will think back to this alliance of two people learning from past mistakes to attempt such a thing: he and Mrs Linde are at once a guarantee that it is possible, and a lesson as to how much it costs emotionally to make this journey.

CHECK THE BOOK

In Act 3 of Ibsen's last play, *When We Dead Awaken* (1899), there is a scene in which two people with a hard experience of relationships – the spouse of an idealistic artist returning to his first model and an embittered hunter – come together, like Nils Krogstad and Mrs Linde, to 'stitch our tattered lives together'.

PART THREE

CRITICAL APPROACHES

CHARACTERISATION

CHECK THE BOOK

Harold Clurman's *Ibsen* (1977) covers all the major plays and also contains advice for students wishing to approach them as a director, explaining how to make preliminary notes.

It took Ibsen twelve months to plan *A Doll's House*, a process he described as one of becoming more closely acquainted with his characters. Writing the first draft, he said, was like meeting them during a railway journey, during which they chatted to him; the second draft was like 'a month spent with them at a spa … I may still be wrong about certain essentials'; the third draft made them 'intimate friends … as I see them now, I shall always see them' (quoted in Clurman, *Ibsen*, 1977, p. 22). All were imagined with a painter's visual flair: he complained of one of the first actresses to play Nora that her hands were the wrong shape. However, his years spent working closely with actors taught him to value their contributions. While reading alone will make it clear that the most trivial exchanges and simple actions convey a weight of unspoken meaning, it is for the performer to decide exactly how and when to make this meaning apparent. In his own lifetime Ibsen could have seen Nora dance the tarantella with passion or in a state of numbed exhaustion; a Helmer in late middle age or one whose pomposity was sharply at odds with his youthful good looks. All the characters should be understood as vehicles for experienced actors – not fixed entities but opportunities to make choices. The cultural climate and the political, social or geographical circumstances in which these choices are made will all yield different readings. All of them will offer something new to their audiences and bring the pages to life in a new way.

NORA

Nora is one of the longest and most complex female dramatic roles, and Ibsen's characterisation was often misunderstood by his early audiences. The early nineteenth century perceived 'character' as a fixed set of traits peculiar to the individual and displayed with consistency throughout the **narrative**. They might learn from experience, but they did not take charge of their own growth as Nora chooses to do. The change from the flighty girl of Act 1 to the sober figure seated at the table with Helmer in Act 3 seemed

incredible. (As recently as 1977 the American director Harold
Clurman admitted in his study of Ibsen that for a long time he had
seen it as a flaw in the play.) Throughout the action, however, we
see latent strengths in Nora; the real energy of the play lies in her
process of self-discovery.

Ibsen rapidly establishes Nora as a figure with great zest for life:
she takes pleasure in the Christmas tree, the taste of macaroons and
champagne. She is physically expressive and at ease, frequently
touching and kissing Helmer affectionately and playing with her
children (given the restrictions of nineteenth-century clothing for
women, this suggests she is quite athletic). Her instinct is to reach
out to people, and we see her embrace the nurse, Mrs Linde and Dr
Rank. She has a kind of natural democracy; her cheerful admission
that she preferred the talk of the servants in her father's house is a
refreshing contrast to her husband's bluster about Krogstad's use of
Christian names.

All this not only endears her to the audience but means that she is
constantly seen in motion; her physical vitality reflects the dynamic
nature of her inner journey. Nora's tarantella also makes clear that
she has the instincts of a natural performer, turning to dance as a
means of expressing what she cannot say; this alerts us to her
dawning awareness that she is 'performing' the role of wife which
society has scripted for her. The Nora perkily acting out the role of
'skylark' or 'squirrel' in Act 1 may well enjoy the game and even the
power she has to wheedle money out of Helmer by *playing with his
waistcoat buttons*' (Act 1, p. 150). But already she thinks this is a
precarious power that will wane 'When I'm not pretty any more'
(Act 1, p. 161), and at some point she may feel resentment at the
'tricks' (Act 2, p. 187 and Act 3, p. 226) she has to perform in order
to ask Helmer for anything – her predicament is, after all, the result
of his stubborn refusal to look after his health. The actress playing
Nora has considerable freedom in deciding how and when she will
make this apparent. The conversation with Mrs Linde, in which
Nora expresses her pleasure in 'working and earning money … like
being a man' (Act 1, p. 162), may trigger new feelings in Nora about
the flattery she uses moments later to get her friend a job at the
bank – feelings which the performer can reflect in her face.

**CHECK
THE BOOK**

Ibsen read Madame
de Staël's novel
Corinne (1807), a
story of doomed
love between the
free-spirited,
passionate Corinne
and a reserved
Scottish aristocrat,
while in Rome, and
his choice of Nora's
dance may have
been prompted
by that danced by
the heroine, who
explores the nature
of performance. Her
talent is to make
'the spectators
experience their
own feelings'.
Nora's dance, a
wordless message
about herself as
well as a plot
device, shows that,
like Corinne,
'everything was
language for her'.

CHECK THE BOOK

Ibsen's notes for his first ideas about the play can be found in George Pierce Baker's *Dramatic Technique* (1919).

CONTEXT

Ibsen told friends that Nora's name was actually a pet name, short for 'Leonora'. This means she is never once addressed as an adult in the play.

Alternatively the actress may prefer to express Nora's disquiet later, in the scene where she tries to introduce the topic of Krogstad while coyly requesting help with her fancy dress. Her **body language** and facial expression, unseen by Helmer as she dresses the Christmas tree, may indicate dislike for the 'performance' she is giving.

But at some point, Nora's feelings and her outward behaviour start to be at odds. Ibsen's 'Notes for the Tragedy of Modern Times', his first jottings towards the play, indicate that he was interested in the idea of 'two kinds of conscience, one for men and one, quite different, for women' (quoted in Egil Törnqvist, *A Doll's House*, 1995, p. 15; Michael Meyer, *Ibsen*, 1985, p. 321). But while Helmer is governed by the rules of society and Nora habitually follows her heart, it could be argued that neither of them has a conscience adequate to make them rational and ethical human beings at the beginning of the play. It is clear from the care with which the text imparts an understanding of Nora's background that she is a product of her upbringing and its limitations. Her naivety in assuming that the law will 'understand' her **motivation**, her snobbish attitude to Krogstad and her smug refusal to consider the problems of 'strangers' (Act 1, p. 149) are not attractive qualities, but they stem from an ignorance of the world that, by the end of the play, she intends to put right. She is aware that she knows nothing beyond the 'play-room' (Act 3, p. 226) which both her father and Helmer have seen as her natural sphere.

Central to Nora's developing self-awareness is the idea of authenticity. She is shocked at Helmer's strictures on 'lying mothers' (Act 1, p. 179) because she has just had a rude awakening from Krogstad about the law's view of forgery. Rapidly she becomes obsessed with the idea that she might 'poison' (p. 180) the minds of her own children; and at once, she does what she feels is right and cuts herself off from them. But although Helmer's point strikes home, she does not instantly manage to link the idea of lying to the way in which she 'performs' the role of submissive wife or dancing temptress as a substitute for expressing her true feelings. Her upbringing in the 'doll's house' has taught her to see this kind of role playing as a way of making her marriage work. It never occurs to her that it actually damages her relationship with Helmer.

Alongside this socially constructed femininity, however, Nora has a desire to do right. She has acted decisively to save her husband's life; she does what she can for Mrs Linde. And in her relationship with Dr Rank she passes from sexual manipulativeness to honesty, at some cost to herself. It is clear that by the middle of Act 2, when she considers asking Dr Rank for help only to desist as soon as he declares his love, she is making an ethical choice: she will betray neither her marriage nor the integrity of Rank's love by asking for money. After this, she finds it almost impossible to return to her old behaviour with Helmer: the tarantella is a more complex message than her usual flatteries. Her faith that Helmer will prove his love by attempting to take the blame on himself is a product of sentimental social conditioning (his as well as hers); but her behaviour with Rank is honourable and tactful and entitles her to expect more from Helmer than hypocritical cowardice.

By the end of the play, Nora is aware that her personality has been largely constructed by others – by the men who love her, and beyond that by a **hegemony** of male authority from the law to the Church. To all of them she has been an object to be played with or looked at; in order to become a subject, she must shape a new self. Her plans have the same clear-sightedness as her farewell to Dr Rank. She replaces fantasies of marital heroism with modest expectations. The decision to stay the night with Mrs Linde and find work (presumably of the kind she has already been doing) indicates that she does not expect her life to be better than that of her old school friend. She is also profoundly aware of the emotional costs. She has already made the break with her children; now she also considers that neither she nor Helmer feels real love for the other. She pays tribute to his kindness, admits that she will 'often think of' him, and in her wry response to his suggestion that they could live as brother and sister – 'You know quite well that that wouldn't last' – even implies that her desire for him has not died (Act 3, p. 231). But for the first time she speaks of 'duty' (Act 3, p. 228) rather than simply of love; she has become a person with the beginnings of a considered moral code rather than loving instincts.

At the start of the play Nora gravitates to the warmth and safety of the stove. When facing the dilemma posed by Dr Rank's declaration

CHECK THE BOOK

Angela Carter's short story 'The Loves of Lady Purple', from her collection *Fireworks* (1974), tells the story of a female puppet who steals life from her maker and walks out into the night; but, because she can only conform to the way she is constructed, she heads for the city brothel.

of love she calls for light; in the last act she is herself a giver of light. Ibsen once remarked to a woman who likened herself to Nora because she had run away with her lover: 'My Nora went alone.' It is Nora's unflinching solitude at the end of the play that marks her, with all her faults, as a heroine unique in her century.

HELMER

CHECK THE BOOK

Charles Dickens, whose novels Ibsen enjoyed, experienced poverty like Ibsen as a result of his father's financial incompetence. Peter Ackroyd's biography shows how the famous lines of Mr Micawber in *David Copperfield* – 'Annual income twenty pounds, annual expenditure nineteen nineteen six, result happiness. Annual income twenty pounds, annual expenditure twenty pounds ought and six, result misery' (Chapter 12) – were originally said by Dickens's father when in Marshalsea Prison for debt (*Dickens*, 1990, p. 71).

It is sometimes difficult for a twenty-first-century audience to realise that as nineteenth-century husbands go, Torvald Helmer is not an unappealing prospect. Even on the point of leaving, Nora says, 'you've always been so kind to me' (Act 3, p. 229). He is sober (unlike Knud Ibsen, Ibsen's father) and industrious almost to a fault, overworking himself to the point of illness in order to achieve promotion and provide for his family. He is gentle: in an age where marital violence was barely considered grounds for divorce, he never attempts to harm Nora even when enraged. His horror of debt seems neurotic in its intensity. Even if he was not aware his illness could be fatal, a holiday in a warmer climate was a standard prescription and most men in his position would not have hesitated to borrow the fare; it suggests that his homily to Nora – 'suppose I borrowed a thousand kroner today and you went and spent it all by Christmas, and then on New Year's Eve a tile fell on my head' (Act 1, p. 148) – expresses real anxiety as well as playful exaggeration. Such anxiety was not uncommon in the nineteenth century: welfare systems were embryonic, and if rapid industrial growth could bring vast fortunes it could also bring terrible losses. In spite of this Helmer, to his credit, can still be generous: Nora seems genuinely pleased with the amount of money he gives her for Christmas shopping, and he appears to enjoy the prospect of hanging 'something in gold paper' on the Christmas tree (Act 1, p. 180).

Helmer sincerely believes that he loves Nora, and that he and her father are 'The two people who loved you more than anyone else in the world' (Act 3, p. 225). Even when, furious that she has ruined his reputation, he is planning to keep Nora's children from her and preserve only the shell of a marriage for the sake of respectability, he cannot quite manage to say that he no longer cares. She is 'someone I've loved so much – someone I still …' (Act 3, p. 222). He certainly continues to feel desire for her after years of marriage; the repeated allusions to songbirds and squirrels, together with Nora's promise to 'be a fairy and dance on a moonbeam' (Act 2, p. 187), suggest that he often expresses it in a playful spirit. However, he can also be insistent to the point of insensitivity: not only does he enjoy the fantasy that Nora is his new bride as she dances the tarantella, but he continues to try to pursue it and 'be with my darling wife' (Act 3, p. 219) even when they have received the calling cards warning them of Dr Rank's imminent death. Helmer is possessive: he enjoys showing off Nora's beauty – 'worth seeing, if you ask *me*!' (Act 3, p. 212) – but once she has been admired he has little interest in the company of other people. Nora tells Mrs Linde that his desire to 'keep me all to himself' (Act 2, p. 184) has led to a refusal to let her talk about her old friends. And while he clearly trusts his wife to be alone with Rank, Helmer also reflects, after learning that they will no longer see him, how good it is 'now that you and I have no one but each other' (Act 3, p. 219).

Helmer's **tragedy** is that he does not know himself. He is clearly intelligent enough to succeed as a barrister and a bank manager, but both are professions in which the rules of conduct are clearly laid down. He enforces these rules and, as Nora says, 'won't touch any case that isn't absolutely respectable' (Act 1, p. 155). This convinces him that he is a person of integrity, entitled to sit in judgement on a man like Krogstad. In fact he is simply a conformist: it does not occur to him to question the rules of society, and he is notably absent from the debate about moral health and the community in Act 1 (p. 165). A real concern for ethics might lead him to condemn Nora; a focus on Christian mercy (he feels that religion should shape her conduct) might lead him to understand that she acted out of love. Instead he gives her no opportunity to explain herself, and it is **ironically** only with Krogstad that she can discuss the complexity of her **motivation**. Helmer appears to have been willing to bend the rules to help Nora's father in the past (see Act 2, pp. 187–8), and has evidently never been found out; when he thinks he is in the power of Krogstad as a result of Nora's forgery, his chief concern is for how he will appear to others. Though his real preoccupation is with reputation, not morality, he seems blind to this distinction: when Nora condemns his refusal to reinstate Krogstad because he dislikes being addressed by his Christian name, Helmer is comically but

CHECK THE NET

You can read a selection of Ibsen's poetry on the Poetry Archive website at **www.poetry-archive.com**

QUESTION

The opening lines of Leo Tolstoy's *Anna Karenina* (1875–8) are: 'All happy families are alike. Every unhappy family is unhappy in its own way.' What is the relationship between family happiness and individualism in *A Doll's House*?

quite genuinely shocked. It does not occur to him that he is being 'petty' rather than exercising legitimate authority (Act 2, p. 189).

In the same way he takes the rules of society for granted, Helmer also assumes that a significant title – such as 'husband' or 'employer' – endows him with a kind of wisdom that cannot be questioned. He issues orders about the use of Christian names, the eating of macaroons or the way to dance the tarantella with absolute confidence in his expertise. He perceives himself as a man of culture and education – an idealist, in fact. He feels competent to stage-manage Nora's dance and lecture Mrs Linde about the relative aesthetic effects of a woman knitting or embroidering. This conviction persists through all the traumas of the final act; he is still confident that he can educate his wife into a new maturity, announcing, 'Play-time's over, now comes lesson-time' (Act 3, p. 226). He never realises that he is more interested in power than in the rights and wrongs of a situation; Nora is almost bitter about his refusal to pander to her '"whims and fancies"' (Act 1, p. 161) by taking the Italian holiday – which he never actually admits was responsible for his present blooming health.

Phrases such as 'We won't have any melodrama' (Act 3, p. 220) and 'No rhetoric, please!' (Act 3, p. 221) suggest that Helmer imagines himself to stand for common sense and plain speaking. In reality he is as prone to self-dramatisation as Nora. His remark that 'I've often wished that you could be threatened by some imminent danger so that I could risk everything I had – even my life itself – to save you' (Act 3, p. 219) conforms to a stereotyped image of masculine heroism straight out of Scribe. The pose comically disintegrates as he reads Krogstad's letter and cries, 'I'm saved!' (Act 3, p. 222), but he rapidly adopts a new posture, that of the forgiving spouse, in which he luxuriates in an embarrassingly prolonged scene of reconciliation and forgiveness rather than simply offering to forget the past. His chosen **imagery** – 'I shall protect you like a hunted dove that I've saved from the talons of a hawk' (Act 3, p. 224) – contrasts absurdly with the craven egotism of 'I'm saved!' He has not learned from his experience but instead uses it to convince himself that he is the saviour in this situation. While by the end of Act 3 Nora is able to look back more coolly on her expectation that he would take the blame on himself, Helmer continues to trot out another cliché of melodrama: 'no man would sacrifice his *honour* for the one he loves' (p. 230) – a phrase generally applied to situations more perilous and complex than the forging of a signature.

Helmer is probably the least admirable character in the play and is clearly self-centred. However, if he is contrasted with a more obvious **villain**, such as the murderous husband in Patrick Hamilton's *Gaslight* (1939), it is plain that he is not consciously selfish in seeking his own gain at the expense of others. For him – as for many a nineteenth-century man secure in his privileged status as bourgeois male – getting his own way is synonymous with doing the right thing. While he sings the virtues of honesty and condemns both Krogstad and 'lying mothers' (Act 1, p. 179), he is blissfully unaware of how powerfully he is protected from harsh realities: his doctors keep his illness from him, his friend will not expose him to the horrors of his deathbed, and his wife even bustles Mrs Linde out of the room so that he will not have to see her sewing. Nora has learned how to flatter and cajole him; in a domestic setting he enjoys this process and gives way – over the Christmas money for example. Sometimes he seems unaware that he has been manipulated: he sees his decision to employ Mrs Linde as a result of her arriving 'at just the right moment' (Act 1, p. 167). Nora would rather lie to him than challenge him, even over something as trivial as a bag of macaroons. This might prompt the audience to indignation on his behalf if he were ever shown making a rational choice; in fact, whenever Helmer acts for himself, it is on very confused moral grounds. Sometimes it is out of childish spite, like his dismissal of Krogstad; or from panicky concern for his own reputation, as when he discovers Nora's crime. He is, in fact, more pampered and indulged than Nora herself, a 'doll' protected from reality – by women out of deference to his masculinity; by men out of concern for his weakness.

Ibsen does not specify Helmer's age, but his first choice for the Swedish production of *A Doll's House* was the handsome young matinee idol Gustaf Fredricksen. If Helmer is played by a young actor, some of the phrases he uses – like his assertion that to forgive

CHECK THE BOOK

You can read the synopses of many of the other plays mentioned in these Notes in *The Oxford Dictionary of Plays*, by Michael Patterson (2005). This is an accessible guide to some of the most popular and significant plays in theatrical history. Each entry has a concise summary of the plot, together with brief commentaries on context and performance history.

CONTEXT

One of the most notorious of all theatrical flops was *A Doll's Life*, a sequel to *A Doll's House* by the highly regarded team Betty Comden and Adolph Green (book and lyrics) and Larry Grossman (music). A fantasy in which Nora tries a number of occupations – scullery maid, wardrobe assistant and mistress to a wealthy man – before returning to talk at the table with Helmer about her experiences, it features numbers such as 'Learn to Be Lonely'. It opened at the Mark Hellinger Theatre in New York on 23 September 1982, and closed three days later.

his wife will make her 'both his wife and his child' (Act 3, p. 224) – will emphasise the play-acting element in his character and the naivety that goes with it. It helps the actor to develop the comic aspects of the role – and it is rare for an audience not to feel some affection for a figure of fun. While Helmer has not outgrown his posturing and pomposity at the end of the play, it is worth noting that he no longer fusses about his own reputation but only about Nora's feelings for him. Perhaps it is still possible that he can change and that the 'greatest miracle of all' (Act 3, p. 232) will occur.

MRS LINDE

Kristina Linde is a quiet and polite woman who is qualified to work in a bank. It is clear that the actress is expected to play her as less blooming than Nora, who finds her pale, thin and not at once recognisable as her old school friend. She is even a little frail, telling Dr Rank that she has to take the stairs 'very slowly' (Act 1, p. 164) and is feeling the strain of overwork. At this stage it seems that she is primarily a **foil** to Nora; she speaks of a hard life which she has clearly borne courageously, but there is no sense that she experienced any interior conflict over her marriage of convenience. Her air of tired experience makes Nora seem empty-headed in comparison – although far livelier and a more entertaining companion.

If Mrs Linde is a little patronising with remarks such as 'a little bit of sewing and that sort of thing!' (Act 1, p. 158), she perhaps has a right to be, although, if the actress so chooses, she may also imply a degree of envy: anyone in Mrs Linde's position might covet children of her own and generous spending money, even if Nora has had to sacrifice the latter temporarily. Helmer clearly finds her worthy but dull, and she seems content that this is so, grateful for the job he has offered. As she interrogates Nora about the loan, her curiosity seems to be simply that of a concerned friend – essentially fulfilling the function of a **confidante** in allowing vital information to emerge. Her kindness is apparent in her concern for 'moral invalid[s]' (Act 1, p. 165) in her debate with Dr Rank. This is, however, allied to stern moral principles; Mrs Linde is worried that Nora's naivety may lead her into a sexual scrape over the loan, which she imagines is from Dr Rank. Her determination to help is strong – she firmly maintains that Krogstad 'must ask for his letter back' (Act 2, p. 202) – but she is equally intent on learning the whole truth of the situation and plays a part in helping it to emerge.

Nevertheless, there is a subversive side to this quiet figure. Mrs Linde has a passion for work – it is her 'one great joy' (Act 3, p. 209). This gives her an independence that makes her highly unusual. Helmer, with his dislike of even the sight of a woman doing something useful, like knitting, cannot imagine this kind of female, and she may well serve to fan the flames of Nora's pleasure in being 'almost like' a man (Act 1, p. 162). We also learn in the last act that she is further than Nora on the road to self-determination. Not only has she chosen the partner of her future life in Krogstad, but she has no shame in telling him that she has come miles especially to find him and propose that they 'join forces' (Act 3, p. 209). Fully aware of what he has done, she is also certain of her own ability to see the best in him and help him change his life. She wants to be a mother, and she will mother his children. Mrs Linde, in short, has already made herself an individual capable of choice. She has, as she bitterly explains, exercised that capability previously, when she first rejected Krogstad for a wealthier man to help her mother and brothers. She cannot say for certain whether it was the right choice – as she admits, 'I've often asked myself … I really don't know' (Act 3, p. 208). But she is clear that 'when you've sold yourself once for the sake of others, you don't do it a second time' (Act 3, p. 210).

Mrs Linde, therefore, is not the passive victim she appeared in Act 1: she owns her experience and the self it has made her. It is this, perhaps, that makes her so determined that there should be 'complete understanding' (Act 3, p. 211) between Nora and Helmer. She may want to shake them both out of dependency – Nora on her ability to lie and perform 'tricks' (Act 2, p. 187 and Act 3, p. 226) to keep her marriage tranquil, and Helmer on the myth of Nora's helplessness. The actress may locate her **motivation** for telling Krogstad to leave his letter in the box in envy, or excessive optimism, or genuine benevolence, but in any case she will prove the deceptively dull Mrs Linde to be one of the most vital and active characters in the play.

CHECK THE BOOK
J. M. Barrie's play *The Twelve-Pound Look* (1910) is the story of a downtrodden wife who has a life-changing encounter with her husband's secretary. She discovers that for twelve pounds, the cost of a typewriter, she can achieve independence. In this play the 'twelve-pound look' in a woman's eye is a dangerous thing.

CONTEXT

The first comprehensive collection of Ibsen's work in English translation was William Archer's *Collected Works of Henrik Ibsen*, published in twelve volumes over six years from 1906 to 1912. One of the most influential theatre critics of his day, Archer was a prolific translator. Bilingual – his grandparents lived in Norway – he was responsible for introducing English audiences to Ibsen with his translations of *The Pillars of Society* (1880) and *A Doll's House* (1889); *Ghosts* and *Hedda Gabler* followed in 1891. He produced a number of books, including *Masks or Faces?* (1888) about the psychology of acting, and *Play-Making* in 1912.

KROGSTAD

Krogstad's name means 'crooked', and his function in the external aspects of the plot is that of a stock **villain**: many of the early Krogstads found themselves unable to play the part any other way. But in terms of the psychological development of the play, Krogstad is a complex figure. Nora rejects the idea that he resembles her, despite their similar crimes, because she cannot imagine his motives to have been 'brave' like hers (Act 1, p. 175). However, his unwillingness to go into the question is not furtive but a clear-sighted recognition that what matters in the world is not motive but the fact of transgression. What he has forfeited by his action is the appearance of respectability in a world run by men like Helmer, to whom appearance is everything. Krogstad has been working on the edge of legality. The agreement he has drawn up with Nora is clearly legally binding, but he has carefully not asked too many questions about the name on the note, or about the fact that a woman (with no right to sign the note herself) has been engaged in the business. Harassing a client, as he does Nora, may be routine in his role as loan shark. Certainly he seems to have the status of a pariah – even the disinterested Dr Rank knows and disapproves of what he does.

Krogstad does not see Helmer as a moral superior; indeed, as the play progresses he seems increasingly to despise him, aware that Helmer will go to considerable lengths to preserve his respectability. But he is driven by a powerful motive to make himself like Helmer: his sense of fatherhood. His determination to 'fight to keep my little post at the Bank as I'd fight for my life' comes from a sense of responsibility to his children – as he tells Nora, 'My sons are growing up, and in fairness to them I must try to win back as much respect as I can in the town' (Act 1, p. 172). Helmer preaches to Nora about Krogstad 'poisoning his own children with lies and deceit' (Act 1, p. 179), but his motives for the dismissal are not out of concern for them – as Krogstad remarks, neither Helmer nor Nora expresses any interest in them (see Act 2, p. 198). Tellingly, while Krogstad invariably refers to 'my children', Helmer typically speaks of 'the children' or sometimes 'your [Nora's] children'. It is only when Krogstad is thwarted that his blackmail threats escalate into a demand for a 'better' job (Act 2, p. 199).

The contempt Krogstad increasingly feels towards Helmer, however, is not extended to Nora. He spells out her criminal status to remedy her ignorance rather than to hit back at the snobbish disdain with which she treats him; he is oddly compassionate in his warning against suicide: 'Most of us think of that at first' (Act 2, p. 198). He may be brutal, but it is an apologetic kind of brutality which never reaches the level of Helmer's fit of rage against Nora in Act 3. It takes Krogstad some time to accept that Mrs Linde cares for him. As he says, 'Life has taught me not to believe in fine speeches' (Act 3, p. 209) – which one can well believe after he has been exposed to so many by Helmer. Once secure in the knowledge he is loved, he is decisive, immediately returning Nora's note of hand. Given that this now means he has no evidence of the loan, he is reaching out to the person whom he has seen throughout the play as his double – Nora – at some cost to himself. If it also benefits the man for whom he has such contempt, his admirable lack of bitterness appears to accept this.

DR RANK

In Act 1 the witty and urbane doctor virtually quotes a writer much admired by Ibsen – Voltaire – when describing Krogstad: 'He's rotten to the core, but the first thing he said – as if it were something really important – was that he must live' (p. 165). This suggests that Dr Rank shares Voltaire's cynical approach to life and that his function in the play is to act as a detached observer, possibly offering advice to the **protagonists** but doing little to change the course of the action – a role familiar in **well-made plays** and one often given to a doctor as the wise man of the community. His discussion with Mrs Linde, in which he complains that in a society obsessed with caring for the morally sick 'The honest man probably finds himself left out in the cold' (Act 1, p. 165), makes him seem both harsh and flippant, yet quite impersonal, as if he enjoys argument for its own sake. It is not until the second act, when Nora mentions his hereditary illness, that we realise Rank himself is just such an 'honest man', cut off from participating fully in life because of the moral sickness of his father. The mental and physical pain of his disease is clearly on his mind all the time – Mrs Linde alludes to his depression during the Christmas celebration we do not see – but it is only occasionally that he articulates his feelings about it.

> **CONTEXT**
>
> François-Marie Arouet (1694–1778), better known by the pseudonym Voltaire, was a French **Enlightenment** writer much admired by Ibsen. A vocal supporter of social reform, he spoke out despite strict censorship laws and harsh penalties for those who broke them. He frequently made use of his works to criticise Church dogma and the French institutions of his day. When a man asked for him for money 'Because I have to live', he replied: 'I don't see the necessity.'

Helmer, presumably, is no more capable of dealing with such emotions in his 'poor old friend' (Act 3, p. 219) than he is with the physical aspects of Rank's disintegration. Rank seems to bear no malice about this limitation in his friend, and the hedonistic front he keeps up before Helmer probably reflects the spirit in which he attempts to approach the time he has left: 'Why shouldn't one enjoy everything the world has to offer – at any rate, as much as one can – and for as long as one can?' (Act 3, p. 216).

Only to Nora does Rank articulate the real depth of his bitterness and rage. Unlike anyone else in the play, she shares his ability to play with language; at times they slip into private codes with the ease of professional comedians. When they indulge in bawdy innuendo with the stockings, it is this sense of being a double act that seems the real source of their pleasure. Humour not only allows Rank to discuss the forbidden subject of his illness, but it also reflects his sense that this is appropriate because 'the whole thing's nothing but a joke!' (Act 2, p. 192). He evidently draws no comfort from religion or philosophy; what he does value is the sense of belonging, of not being out in the cold, and he expresses a real need to retain till the end his place in the Helmer household. Nora determinedly adds a reminder that he is 'at home with *us*' (Act 2, p. 193; my italics) rather than 'me', and his affection for Helmer is clear – but it is also clear that Rank cherishes a fantasy of being Nora's husband. His devotion is rooted in more than desire, and we have no reason to suppose he is not perfectly sincere in his wish to 'give his life' for her (Act 2, p. 194).

If Rank does not radically affect the action of the play, this is not because he wants to settle for the role of observer; he is deprived of the chance to help Nora by her own sense of moral responsibility, just as he is deprived by his illness of leaving behind much more than 'a passing regret' (Act 2, p. 194).

THE NURSE (ANNA-MARIA)

Although she has few lines, the role of the nurse is important. We first see her surrounded by happy children (Act 1, p. 168): it is clear that she is good at her job, and Nora's concern at how cold she is suggests that Anna-Maria is more interested in the children's

> **CONTEXT**
>
> The practice of wet-nursing (employing a woman to breastfeed a child not her own) is very ancient – Tutankhamen buried his with honour – and the figure of the nurse as **confidante** is common in literature of all periods. One of the most famous is the nurse in Shakespeare's *Romeo and Juliet* (c.1595), who plays a major part in the action. The role of nurse generally stands for rough common sense.

enjoyment than her own comfort. She may well see herself as the most authoritative figure in the nursery – Nora asks to be allowed to take off the children's coats as a kind of treat rather than assuming that she can do so. She is clearly aware of the boundaries between servant and mistress; although obviously concerned when Nora begins to avoid the children, she asks no questions. However, there is evident affection between Nora and the nurse – to all intents and purposes, as she says, Nora 'hadn't any other mother but me', and Nora thinks that she has been 'wonderful' in this role (Act 2, p. 182).

It is the nurse who is probably responsible for the fact that Nora feels most comfortable with people who are not authority figures, such as her father's servants or Dr Rank. The pride she feels in Nora's beauty as they get her costume ready for the party suggests that her motherly feelings are still very much alive. So does her response to Nora's peevishness about the state of her fancy dress – the nurse will not countenance its wasteful destruction and says reprovingly, 'it only needs a little patience' (Act 2, p. 181). The actress playing her may choose to develop the subtext of this to suggest a concern for Nora's marriage. Whether or not Anna-Maria is aware of the situation, it is clear that Nora trusts her old nurse to bring up her children in her absence. The audience's response to the nurse will be important in the final act; although she does not appear, we will judge Nora on leaving her children less harshly if it is clear they are in good hands.

Of all the characters in *A Doll's House*, Anna-Maria has suffered the most. She has known poverty and disgrace. Betrayed by 'that blackguard of a man' (Act 2, p. 182), she had no option but to give up her own child. Her suffering contrasts sharply with that of the main characters, whose concern is ultimately over a piece of paper. Even Krogstad has managed to keep his children. The dignity and optimism with which she has made a new life and accepts its limitations provide a clear comment on Nora and Helmer's future prospects: it is possible to change and live differently, but it is also undeniable that the world can be a harsh and unforgiving place.

> **CONTEXT**
>
> Else Jensdatter, the mother of Ibsen's illegitimate son Hans Jacob Henriksen, was already impoverished when he met her, her grandfather having lost the family fortune by leading an uprising against the Danes. On becoming pregnant, she had to give up her work as a maid. Although Ibsen made her an allowance and her son became a blacksmith, she never recovered her place in society and died in a small hut in the hills as a pauper in 1892.

THEMES

THE INDIVIDUAL AND SOCIETY

A doll is not a person. Its character is determined by its owner according to what functions it is expected to serve: baby or fashion model for example. It does not have a role in public – even small children do not generally take their dolls to school. When Nora claims that 'before everything else I'm a human being' (Act 3, p. 228), she is also claiming the right to make a self. Although Ibsen professed not to have read his work, the issues at stake for Nora reflect the ideas of the Danish philosopher Søren Kierkegaard (1813–55), sometimes known as the father of **existentialism**. Existentialism is the idea that a person is not born with innate characteristics but shapes a self through the choices that they make. For Kierkegaard this process was threatened by taking any religious or philosophical creed for granted. It was vital to understand that the individual was free to choose his or her beliefs and actions. Once this was understood, it was possible to shape the self by exercising personal responsibility in making such choices.

At the beginning of the play Nora's identity is determined by others. For Helmer she is a pet animal, a sexual partner, a mother and a housekeeper, and we see her adopt all these roles as necessity arises. She makes one choice – in forging her father's name – but it is instinctive and, significantly, secret. She assumes it will have no effect on *who she is* (despite committing forgery she cannot conceive of herself as a criminal) as long as it remains so. Engagement with the world outside the home is a form of play or disguise: 'being a man' (Act 1, p. 162). She has no sense of responsibility towards 'strangers' (Act 1, p. 149), a term which includes creditors and even Krogstad and his children. Her lack of interest in 'your dreary old community' (Act 1, p. 165) means that she does not participate in the debate between Mrs Linde and Dr Rank as to how the world is or should be organised. For many nineteenth-century thinkers this would have been understandable: it was for the male to achieve self-definition through 'struggle with the external world and with himself' (Toril Moi, *Henrik Ibsen and the Birth of Modernism: Art, Theater, Philosophy*, 2006, p. 245),

CONTEXT

Kierkegaard was a prolific writer combining philosophy, theology, psychology, literary criticism, devotional literature and fiction. Through this mixture of disciplines he explored the notion of personal responsibility. He remained a Christian, although many of his followers did not. Ibsen may have read *Either/Or*, which appeared in 1843; his mother-in-law, Magdalene Thoresen, certainly had.

while the status of 'wife' or 'mother' expressed a particular *function* – to care for the husband and give birth to and bring up children – rather than a set of choices through which a woman might become an individual in her own right.

Act 2, however, marks Nora's dawning awareness that the most private choices have wider moral implications. She realises that while Dr Rank could save the situation, without Helmer's knowledge, choosing to take his money would redefine their relationship as one grounded in power, not affection. In acting as a morally responsible individual Nora throws into relief Helmer's panic at the sight of Krogstad's letter: her husband is neither instinctively heroic nor honest enough to make a moral choice. Instead he opts to appease Krogstad while preserving a respectable facade which will involve Nora *acting out* the roles of wife and mother. Once 'saved' (Act 3, p. 222), he thinks he can grant her the real roles once more – indeed, he thinks them her 'sacred duties' (Act 3, p. 227). But Nora can no longer accept him as spokesman for the powerful forces in society that have failed her: as a lawyer he fostered her ignorance of the law; in appealing to religion he is a hypocrite – significantly he calls it 'your religion' (Act 3, p. 228), as if it is not something men need. She cannot allow him to define wifehood or motherhood, but plans to learn for herself. Already beginning to shape an individual self beyond these generic roles, she will find her own moral code in the 'community': that is, with the help of Mrs Linde, now inextricably linked to the former 'stranger' Krogstad; and in her 'old home' (Act 3, p. 227) – not in the role of daughter, as her parents are dead, but as a woman in a 'community' where she can work and learn.

DEATH, DISEASE AND HEREDITY

'Well, I must take you as you are – it's in your blood. Oh yes, Nora, these things are hereditary', announces Helmer in response to Nora's first request for money (Act 1, p. 151), and by the end of the play he is convinced that 'all your father's shiftless character has come out in you. No religion, no morality, no sense of duty' (Act 3, p. 221). He never wavers from his conviction – shared by many in the new world of Charles Darwin – that moral as well as physical qualities can be inherited. Between these two statements, however,

> **CONTEXT**
>
> Criminological research at this period indicated that the young were not corrupted by lying mothers but by poverty and homelessness. A report by James Greenwood in 1869 stated: 'daily, winter and summer, within the limits of [the] city of London, there wander, destitute of proper guardianship, food, clothing, or employment, a hundred thousand boys and girls in fair training for the treadmill … and … the convict's mark' (*The Seven Curses of London*).

we have learned that Nora is only pretending to share her father's extravagance: the money she appears to be wasting goes towards her debt to Krogstad. And while her father may have been knowingly involved in fraud or corruption, her 'crime' is due to ignorance. She says, defiantly, that 'I wish I'd inherited more of papa's good qualities' (Act 1, p. 151), but we do not know what these might be – Helmer never names them and perhaps does not like to discuss the subject. For Helmer 'inheritance' seems to deny the individual any possibility of self-transformation. This former barrister does not appear to believe that one can choose to obey the law, or even to disobey it, on moral grounds; criminality is in the blood or not.

CONTEXT

Ibsen had been interested in the theme of inherited illness since his friend Georg Brandes encountered the David family in 1866. Caroline David was married to a man she claimed had a sexually transmitted disease. Brandes was convinced that her husband was also her half-brother, a theme Ibsen explored along with that of syphilis in *Ghosts* (1881).

The one figure entitled to speak with authority on heredity, the doctor of medicine, is also its victim. Nora passes judgement on the man responsible for his plight: 'his father was a horrible man who had mistresses and that sort of thing' (Act 2, p. 184). Dr Rank, on the other hand, is surprisingly forgiving, referring to his father merely as a 'gay young subaltern' (Act 2, p. 192). The anger that he does feel is not purely for himself but at the injustice of hereditary disease – that 'there isn't a single family where some such inexorable retribution isn't being exacted' (Act 2, p. 192). However, Rank's inheritance is biological, not moral. He seems to have remained unmarried, so that his illness will die with him. His love for Nora is proclaimed when he has 'less than a month' (Act 2, p. 191) to live and could never act on it – indeed, he only presumes to use the word in the past tense: 'To have loved you as deeply as anyone else – was that horrid?' (Act 2, p. 195). He stands, in fact, as a visible repudiation of all Helmer's theories about Nora's father, although Helmer cannot see it.

Both Helmer and Rank use the **metaphor** of corrupt behaviour as moral sickness. But for Helmer this sickness invariably spreads, and its source is the home; he instructs Nora about 'lying mothers' who infect their houses and their children with 'the germs of evil' (Act 1, p. 179), presumably reinforcing the work of heredity. Rank uses the expression 'a moral invalid' but sees it as denoting an individual, to whom society should act with limited compassion; he has little patience with Mrs Linde's argument that society has a responsibility to care for those 'sick' in this way (Act 1, p. 165). But although Mrs

Linde and Dr Rank never continue their discussion, Krogstad's redemption by Mrs Linde forms a coda to this argument with a clear indication that moral sickness can be healed.

The play is full of startlingly graphic images of death. Rank describes his own body 'rotting in the churchyard' (Act 2, p. 191), and is in no doubt how appalling the last stage of his illness will be. Nora also intends to die, in water 'black, and cold as ice' (Act 3, p. 220). However, she is not allowed to romanticise this image – Krogstad's mocking evocation of her corpse floating up bald and hideous in the thaw takes care of that (Act 2, p. 200). Krogstad and Helmer – with the latter's rather selfish point that her suicide wouldn't help *his* reputation – for all their differences, share the opinion that suicide is not a noble sacrifice, even if it constitutes an admission of responsibility. The play moves the audience too towards that unidealist conclusion. Dr Rank's final resentment at leaving his life without even being able to offer 'the smallest token of gratitude' (Act 2, p. 194) to change the life of someone he loves reminds us that – unlike victims of heredity like Rank – even morally 'sick' individuals such as Krogstad hold the possibility of their own change and cure in their hands as long as they hold on to life.

THEATRICALITY

Ibsen often told his actors to avoid 'theatrical accents' and copy the life they saw around them, not other actors (Toril Moi, *Henrik Ibsen and the Birth of Modernism: Art, Theater, Philosophy*, 2006, p. 116). He wanted his audience to respond to 'Nora' or 'Krogstad' rather than '**ingénue**' or '**villain**'. But Nora and Helmer themselves have to think about the idea of performance. 'Theatrical' in everyday language is often equated with insincerity, lies or transforming the self into a commodity; it is no coincidence that 'actress' was for many years a **euphemism** for 'prostitute'. It is in this spirit that Helmer says, 'We won't have any melodrama' (Act 3, p. 220), because he thinks Nora is being insincere.

However, it is when Nora and Helmer are most conscious that they are performing that they express themselves and their relationships most clearly. The fancy dress party offers a focus for their need to

CHECK THE BOOK
If you wish to find out more about the lives and work of many of the authors mentioned in these Notes, *The Oxford Companion to English Literature*, edited by Margaret Drabble (revised sixth edition, 2006), is a good place to begin.

CONTEXT
The idea of dressing as a fisher-girl suggests the French queen Marie Antoinette's habit of dressing up as a shepherdess and playing at the simple life in a specially constructed palace, Le Petit Trianon, just outside Paris. It suggests the middle-class Helmer has some pretensions to grandeur.

'stage' their lives in order to make sense of them. Throughout the play there is an unspoken debate about the meaning of Nora's Capri dress and the dance she performs in it. Helmer's choice of costume for Nora shows exactly what he wishes her to be: his economic inferior; a **symbol** of his sexual and social status in possessing a beautiful wife (both Rank and Nora are aware of the significance of the silk stockings). Helmer sees Nora's dance as an expression of his own artistic ability; he assumes the role of Pygmalion, the legendary sculptor who produced a statue so beautiful that he fell in love with it and it came to life. He forgets something important about the nature of performance: first, it requires mundane work as well as inspiration (Helmer is offended at the sight of women working, including Mrs Linde mending the dress); second, it involves more than one person in making choices. Nora's dance is an outlet for the panic and terror she feels, and she chooses to dance it in a style Helmer condemns as 'a trifle too realistic' (Act 3, p. 212).

It is after this experience that Nora is able to articulate the role performance has played throughout her married life. Her 'tricks' (Act 2, p. 187 and Act 3, p. 226) – the 'skylark' and 'squirrel' games, the flirtatiousness – are harmless in themselves, but they have allowed her to hide the problems in her marriage from herself as well as her husband. She is no longer quite certain who she is: 'You arranged everything to suit your own tastes, and so I came to have the same tastes as yours … or I pretended to. I'm not quite sure which' (Act 3, p. 226). Rank remarks to Nora that at the next fancy dress party she should play a 'mascot' – a talisman, a bringer of happiness – simply by being herself (Act 3, p. 217). This is a graceful compliment, and an expression of gratitude for what she has meant to him. But it is also a reminder that she is an individual as well as a wife. It is partly through moments like her dance, or through the conscious choice of a garment or a role, that Nora has been able to move from acting out stereotypes to exploring what it means to express herself – to discover who she is 'in her everyday things' (Act 3, p. 224).

MONEY

A Doll's House could be described as the story of twelve hundred dollars. This is the sum that Nora borrows in order to save her

CONTEXT

In Greek mythology, Pygmalion fashioned a statue of a woman so beautiful he fell in love with her. Answering his prayers, the gods brought her to life for him. George Bernard Shaw's play *Pygmalion* (first performed in 1913) shows a professor of phonetics who educates a cockney flower-seller only to find that she has her own ideas about what to do with her life, just as Nora does.

husband's life – in other words, to do something useful. However, within the play this sum is represented not by gold or legal tender but by Nora's note of hand, a piece of paper that is evidence of a crime and a tool for a blackmailer. It stands for pretences, false promises and the misuse of power – a fitting symbol of the Helmer marriage.

Nora's action has made her a criminal. She could not, of course, legally borrow money without Helmer's consent, and could only turn to a lender with a reputation for dishonest dealing. Hence it was inevitable that at some point she would find herself being blackmailed. Krogstad has clearly been suspicious about the signature on the note from the outset. However, her criminal act has also brought her out of the domestic sphere in which she has been confined into a world that is new to her, and she seems to take some pride in this. When she says, defiantly, '*I* wrote Papa's name' (Act 1, p. 175), she is not only admitting forgery but proclaiming her place in a world of '"quarterly payments" and "instalments"' (Act 1, p. 161) – a world which belongs to men alone and in which they do not behave with the honesty that they seem to expect of women.

Helmer is quick to condemn Nora, but she is in this situation because he is afraid of the power of money; although his job at the bank must involve borrowing and lending, he cannot cope with debt even to save his own life. However, in accepting the twelve hundred dollars as a gift from his father-in-law, a man he knew to be involved in underhand financial dealings, Helmer has been more than a little hypocritical. Nora remarks to Mrs Linde that 'Torvald has to live properly' (Act 1, p. 161). This involves some luxuries – the black Havana cigar which Dr Rank requests in Act 3 would not be cheap. While Helmer may talk airily about sacrifices in Act 1, Nora is the one who has had to retrench in order to meet her payments to Krogstad. She struggles to make these honestly. This is all the more difficult because for those closest to her money seems to be inextricably bound up with sexuality. Mrs Linde assumes that the loan has come from Dr Rank. Helmer is generous with the housekeeping but does not seem to regard it as Nora's right as mistress of the household. Rather he views it as something he

 CHECK THE NET
A useful essay on the drama of forgery, money and nineteenth-century economic anxiety is Jane Moody's 'The Drama of Capital: Risk, Belief, and Liability on the Victorian Stage', published in *Victorian Literature and Finance*, edited by Francis O'Gorman (2007, pp. 91–110). To read it online, use a search engine and type in the author and essay title.

enjoys being coaxed into giving, a gift in gold paper rather than a recognition that letting him 'live properly' costs money.

Nobody in the play produces anything of value. Helmer earns his money in a bank, controlling the flow of cash in the community. As a loan shark Krogstad does the same as Helmer, on a rather more dishonest level; all the other characters, with the exception of Dr Rank, are in some way in the service of the bank: as clerks, like Mrs Linde, and Krogstad in his more respectable job; as servants to the bank manager; or, in Nora's case, as his wife. Helmer no longer practises law, and Dr Rank is now unable to practise medicine on anyone but himself. The 'community' which is the subject of debate in Act 1 is controlled by money and debt, and this proves to dominate relationships until the end of the play.

TRANSLATION

CHECK THE BOOK

Weber, who did not know English well and worked with the aid of a dictionary, can sometimes be accidentally illuminating. For example he inadvertently punctures Helmer's sentimental image of Nora as a 'hunted dove' (Act 3, p. 224) by translating it as 'chased pigeon'. You can read more extracts in an essay by William Archer in Michael Egan's *Henrik Ibsen: The Critical Heritage* (1972).

It is worth bearing in mind that no English version of *A Doll's House* will give exactly the sense of Ibsen's *Et dukkehjem*. One translator may make it a priority to be as accurate as possible; another may choose to replicate the impact of the original by finding an English equivalent for a Norwegian slang expression or for the way a Norwegian might address an official like Helmer by the professional title *Direktor*, as Mrs Linde does in Act 3 (in the 1965 Penguin Classics edition used in these Notes, Watts has Mrs Linde calling Helmer 'Mr Helmer', p. 214). Victorian England was fortunate to have the bilingual William Archer to provide a fairly speakable translation; earlier versions were, to say the least, bizarre: one by the Danish schoolteacher T. Weber became notorious – justly, as you can see below. But no translation can be exact, and even the simplest sentence in translation carries a slightly different weight of meaning from the original. While this need not spoil our enjoyment or understanding of a play, it can be interesting to see how different translations shift an emphasis. Take, for example, Nora's final line in Act 3:

'That cohabitation between you and me might become a matrimony. Good-bye.' (T. Weber, translated 1880)

'That communion between us shall be a marriage. Good-bye.'
(William Archer, 1889)
'Where we could make a real marriage of our lives together.
Goodbye!' (James McFarlane, 1961)
'That life together between us two could become a marriage.
Goodbye.' (Michael Meyer, 1965)
'That our life together could be a real marriage. Good-bye.'
(Peter Watts, 1965)

The English playwright, actor and critic Harley Granville-Barker
(1877–1946) offered a prize to any drama student who could say
Weber's line with a straight face, and it is perhaps worth a glance at
Weber to realise that translation involves a great deal more than
looking up words in a dictionary.

The religious and mystical overtones of Archer's 'communion'
suggest that Nora has very high expectations of marriage; for the
translators of the 1960s, when churchgoing had declined, it sounded
too explicitly religious for a woman who had just stated her
intentions to find her own moral pathway rather than rely on
the Church's teaching. By using the plural, 'our lives together',
McFarlane implies that if Nora and Helmer resumed their marriage
their lives would run side by side; even, perhaps, that they would
both have careers. Meyer's 'life together between us two' is more
elaborate than Watts's 'our life together', forcing the actress to slow
the pace of the speech. In doing so, she may sound as if she is
pondering the unlikelihood of the event, while Watts's more concise
Nora may still consider it a possibility. None of these are wrong –
Ibsen's original could carry all these shades of meaning and leave
the performer the choice of how to inflect them – but the process
of choosing a translation can teach the reader a great deal about
the play.

LANGUAGE AND STYLE

In 1883 the Swedish actor-director August Lindberg, the first
person to produce *Ghosts*, received a letter in which Ibsen made his
priorities clear:

 CHECK THE NET
You can read
Archer's translation
of *A Doll's House*
and other Ibsen
plays online at
www.archive.org
– search for
'Collected Works
Ibsen'; *A Doll's
House* can be found
in the seventh
volume.

QUESTION
Choose a speech
in the play that
you admire, and
write your own
paraphrase of it.
Compare your
version with one or
more translations
of the same text.
What differences
of emphasis can
you find?

 CHECK THE NET
Further translations
of *A Doll's House*,
together with many
of Ibsen's other
plays, are available
to read online at
**www.online-
literature.com** and
**www.gutenberg.
org**

The dialogue must seem perfectly natural, and the manner of expression must differ from character to character. Many changes in the dialogue can be made during rehearsals, where one can easily hear what sounds natural and unforced, and also what needs to be revised over and over again until finally it sounds completely real and believable.

(Quoted in J. L. Styan, *Modern Drama in Theory and Practice: Realism and Naturalism*, 1981, p. 28)

 CHECK THE NET

For an overview of the theatre during the nineteenth century and an essay on the development of dramatic literature during this period, together with a brief biography of Ibsen and synopses of his plays, go to **www. theatredatabase. com** and click on '19th Century'.

This was a new way of thinking about dialogue. Earlier nineteenth-century drama was more interested in obtaining emotional effects than in reflecting the rhythms of everyday speech. Ibsen was happy to listen and learn from actors as they relaxed into a role; the freshness this imparted allowed his text to appear as if every line was being spoken for the first time. He had given them a very solid basis on which to work: the characters speak so distinctively that most people faced with some random lines could probably attribute them to the correct speaker. Helmer, for instance, seems almost incapable of even a brief speech without using the **imperative voice** – and he does not make many brief speeches. Nora, even making what must be the most considered statement of her whole life as she leaves him, talks at far less length. She has, however, more variety of tone and mood; her language differs subtly with each person she addresses. The cajoling tone she adopts with Helmer is very different from the brisk and friendly equality apparent in remarks such as: 'You're a fine one, Dr Rank!' (Act 2, p. 195), or from her imperious tone to Krogstad in Act 1. Helmer's language is consistent; he lectures Mrs Linde, for example, just as he does Nora.

One of the most important aspects of vocabulary for Helmer is titles. In nineteenth-century Norway professional titles were regularly used as a form of address, so that Helmer would be addressed as '*Advocat*' (Lawyer) or '*Direktor*' (Bank Manager) Helmer, as Mrs Linde politely calls him in Act 3. Krogstad upsets him by addressing him as '*du*' ('thou') as if they were close friends. There is no exact equivalent of this in English – 'Christian name' does not really reflect the level of familiarity. (One wonders whether Krogstad is doing it to annoy.) Helmer nearly always refers to Nora by a nickname or patronising adjective like 'little' – generally prefaced with a possessive 'my'.

Spontaneity and **colloquial** ease are not easily achieved in **naturalistic** dialogue; the audience has to be given certain information which the characters clearly know already. Ibsen manages it with great economy – for example in the rapidity with which we learn about the family finances through the perfectly natural discussion that arises over the Christmas tree in Act 1. However, Ibsen's language is more complex than this; he was perhaps the first playwright to realise the possibilities of **subtext**, of the energies that pulse beneath the words and come alive through the actors' performance of the text. Sometimes characters are conscious that they mean more than they say: Nora and Dr Rank discuss the forbidden topic of syphilis in language about food, showing not only an awareness of the scandalous nature of the subject but also how they enjoy the closeness of their friendship and the exercise of their wit. But if they are proud of their control of language – as in the way they flirt outrageously over the silk stockings – they can be taken by surprise by their own directness: Rank's declaration of love is something he cannot repress. Finally, in the last act, they say a loving farewell through their **allusions** to 'light' (pp. 217–18). The word has acquired a **symbolism** for them over the three days of the action – although, perhaps, they are still unaware of some of the connotations it will have for us.

While her awareness of multiple layers of language permits Nora to grow, Helmer's rigidity is reflected in the way he takes discussions like these at face value and never looks below the surface of his own language. For instance, he repeatedly employs the endearments 'skylark' and 'squirrel' without reflecting that these are wild creatures – that Nora's domestic setting has become a cage. The audience, however, realises that Helmer has built a kind of linguistic prison, not just for Nora but for himself. He is completely at a loss in their final confrontation, and it is entirely up to her to find language to articulate the possibility of change in their relationship. When Nora expresses a longing to say '"Well I'm damned!"' (Act 1, p. 166), she is being frivolous; but it is also indicates the importance she places on freedom of speech in a house where Helmer's refusals

 CHECK THE BOOK

In Caryl Churchill's play *Cloud Nine* (1979) the downtrodden Victorian wife Betty is played in the first act by a man – as she tells the audience: 'I am a man's creation as you see. And what men want is what I want to be.' Her daughter Victoria is played by a doll, because Victorian girls were meant to be seen and not heard. Only in the second act, when all the characters have shifted into the present day, are Betty and Vicky played by women and shown acting for themselves.

to discuss subjects of importance with her constitute a kind of censorship.

Scattered throughout the play are moments when the language seems to resemble that of the **melodramas** Ibsen despised: in particular, Nora has a number of **soliloquies**, ranging from casual remarks such as 'Yes, he's in' (Act 1, p. 148) to a speech that would not seem out of place in Scribe at the end of Act 2: 'Seven hours till midnight. Then twenty-four hours till midnight tomorrow. Then the tarantella will be over. Twenty-four and seven ... thirty-one hours to live' (p. 206). Ibsen prided himself on getting rid of this device in *The League of Youth* (1869), and it is clear that these moments are not, in plot terms, strictly necessary. However, these speeches tell us something about Nora's imagination. She is behaving as if she is living in a world of melodrama, where men make noble sacrifices for women and women make even nobler ones for men. Ibsen's original audience may have been partially aware that life is not really like that, but their imagination too was very much shaped by those same literary stereotypes. They would probably have been in no doubt that Nora should indeed commit heroic suicide, or be saved by Helmer. When instead she slams the door and walks into an unknown future, she is showing that her understanding of the world has changed and she no longer expects a 'miracle' or a happy ending as if she lived in a world scripted by Scribe – and Ibsen is challenging his audience too to abandon such simplistic expectations of a play.

STRUCTURE

A Doll's House follows Scribe's prescription for a **well-made play** very clearly. The **exposition** sets up the situation; through the conversations in Act 1 with Helmer, Mrs Linde and Nils Krogstad we are supplied with all the information that we need to understand what has already happened, and we are made aware that the situation has become pressing – in fact, Nora can already be said to be in crisis, and the action moves with far greater speed than a nineteenth-century audience would have been expecting. The curtain falls on a note of high suspense with Krogstad's first

CHECK THE BOOK
John Russell Taylor's *The Rise and Fall of the Well Made Play* (1967) usefully discusses the development of the format both before and after the impact of Ibsen, and helps to build a picture of the tastes and expectations of a typical audience. He demonstrates the durability of the structure with its emphasis on **suspense** and an exciting curtain at the end of each act.

demand. The **development and complication** in Act 2 see Nora struggling to find a way out, first by changing Helmer's mind, then by asking for Dr Rank's help, only for the action to reach its major crisis when all her possible solutions fail and Krogstad makes even more serious demands. Nora's desperation – using her tarantella to postpone the inevitable – makes a **strong curtain**. Act 3 drives towards the climax; Ibsen develops the suspense further by hinting at a possible **resolution** – the new-found goodwill of Krogstad could mean that the letter is destroyed – and then teasingly closes that possibility with Mrs Linde's determination to reveal the truth. He builds up further suspense by making Dr Rank delay Helmer's reading of the letter, before reaching what Scribe called the *scène à faire* – the scene the audience has been eagerly expecting and will consider an important part of the evening's entertainment: the confrontation between Nora and Helmer.

At the **denouement**, the revelation of all secrets, the audience are conditioned to expect something like Helmer's luxurious meditation on forgiveness: shockingly, they only get it after his more spontaneous display of selfishness has rendered it meaningless. The resolution, the point at which the well-made play is expected to tie up all loose ends, proves to be a **reversal of expectation**. Nora's quiet announcement that she is leaving her marriage comes like a cold shower; her final exit is not so much an ending as the beginning of a new story.

The play also has a more individual structure, mimicking the changes within Nora's own psyche. The action takes place over three days; frequent reminders of the passage of time increase the suspense. However, each act takes place at a different time of day. Days in a Norwegian winter are very short, and Christmas is close to the shortest day of the year. We may infer that Nora's shopping trip before the curtain rises on Act 1 makes the most of the available daylight and that it is not long after the late morning sunrise. In Act 2 Nora calls for the lamp during her conversation with Dr Rank: it is evidently mid afternoon and growing darker. Act 3 takes place at night: the party upstairs audibly breaks up, suggesting it cannot be much earlier than midnight; the final conversation therefore takes place in the small hours of the next day. Despite the passage of time,

CHECK THE NET
The online Encyclopaedia Britannica has an informative article on Henrik Ibsen that gives an overview of his life and major works. Go to **www.britannica. com** and search for 'Henrik Ibsen'.

CHECK THE BOOK
George Bernard Shaw wrote of this moment: 'the slam of the door behind her is more momentous than the cannon of Waterloo'. You can read this contemporary account of Ibsen's reception in England, and its context, in Shaw's *Our Theatres in the Nineties* (1948, Vol. III, p. 131).

the sense is that Nora is living through a single day; this adds to the pace but, more importantly, gives us the impression of a journey from light into profound darkness – with, perhaps, the hope of a return to the light at the end. The Christmas setting adds to this sense of spiritual death and rebirth; although the possibility of the 'greatest miracle of all' (Act 3, p. 232) seems remote, Nora's own life is beginning anew.

STAGING

CONTEXT

An English pioneer of practical stage furniture was T. W. Robertson (1829–71). He began his career as an actor, but retired from the stage and became a playwright. He favoured real doors that actors could slam with confidence rather than painted images, and a chair or a piano would be incorporated into the action. While his plays such as *Caste* (1867) seem slight, they demand ensemble acting rather than star turns and their characters are recognisable types from the less wealthy London of the day.

Ibsen's advice to writers was 'Use your eyes' (quoted in Michael Meyer, *Ibsen*, 1985, p. 501), and the visual dimension of his play is as important as the lines. Most nineteenth-century theatres had a **proscenium arch** stage, but the actors interacted with the audience, speaking some of their lines directly to them, rather than treating the audience as a fly on an invisible wall; instead of **practical** furniture, sets used a backcloth with everything painted on it. Not only does Ibsen show life going on in the Helmer house as if we are not there to watch, but he uses real objects and gives them significant functions: a piano, a Christmas tree, a lamp, a table where serious conversation takes place. Costume is equally eloquent: the clothing of those with money, Rank and Helmer, differs in quality and function from the dress of Helmer's employees, Krogstad and Mrs Linde. Nora's stylish but comparatively cheap dress and her Capri outfit both demonstrate aspects of her married life – her secret economies and the possessiveness of the man who dresses her like a doll.

Space itself is used to illustrate Nora's journey to independence. The focus is the living room, but there is a way out into the hall and two entrances to Helmer's study. Nora never enters through either of Helmer's doors, and while others come and go freely in the hall she becomes increasingly confined; we see her confidently entering the hall just once, at the rise of the curtain; later she almost isolates herself in the room, sending the children away; and later still she is locked in by Helmer. Her final transit through the house is a slow reclamation of freedom. The script carefully locates the Helmer home in a set of apartments: at the end she leaves the room; we see her pass the self-imposed barrier of the hall; we mark her passage down the stairs and into the outer hall, as Helmer continues to hope she will change her mind; and then, with the last echoing slam of the door, we hear her leave the house.

PERFORMANCE HISTORY

THE FIRST PRODUCTIONS

The first production in Copenhagen in 1879 – appropriately on 21 December – starred Betty Hennings, much loved in **ingénue** roles. Her Nora was above all a child, high-spirited and physically lively (Hennings was a former ballerina and her tarantella technically brilliant). Critics were universal in their praise for the way she handled the transition to the more sober figure of the last act, but the perceptive Brandes also considered that there was a dimension of passion missing which deprived the break-up of the marriage of its real poignancy (as discussed in the chapter 'One Nora, many Noras' in *Ibsen's Lively Art: A Performance Study of the Major Plays* by Frederick J. Marker and Lise-Lone Marker, 1989, p. 50). One of the greatest European actresses to take up the role was Eleonora Duse, whose reading of the character was completely different. Quiet, intense and increasingly exhausted by the weight of her secrets until her Capri dress clashed with an ashen face marked by what Archer called 'the shadow of death' (*Theatrical World*, 1893), Duse cut Nora's romping with the children and reduced the tarantella to a few steps; this was a Nora who had already discovered herself and for whom the ending was inevitable from the outset.

Nora appealed to the imagination of critics, whether they approved of her or not, and they were alert to the possibility of different readings of the character. However, responses to other performers suggested that critics made up their minds before the play began. Helmer was the focus of much sympathy; they felt he had a lot to put up with. Emil Poulsen's Helmer to Hennings's Nora, played without any attempt to court such sympathy, was considered 'coarse' by several critics including the influential Herman Bang, while Krogstad was almost invariably dismissed as a **stock character**: a **villain**.

> **CONTEXT**
>
> Eleonora Duse (1858–1924), known as 'the Duse', was considered by many to be the greatest tragic actress of her day. Her stage presence was restrained and quiet, in comparison with the showier Sarah Bernhardt, her greatest rival, and she never wore make-up on stage. One of her greatest roles was that of Mrs Alving in Ibsen's *Ghosts* (1881).

CONTEXT

Janet Achurch
(1864–1916) was
dubbed by George
Bernard Shaw 'the
only tragic actress
of genius we now
possess'. She was a
noted Cleopatra
for actor-manager
Frank Benson and,
like several of his
famous company
of Shakespearean
actors, is
commemorated
in stained glass
at the Royal
Shakespeare
Theatre in
Stratford-upon-
Avon.

**CHECK
THE BOOK**

As well as
pioneering Ibsen
on the London
stage at her own
expense, Achurch
encouraged Shaw
to write the
controversial
*Mrs Warren's
Profession* (1893),
and wrote a play
herself on the
subject of
prostitution,
*Mrs Daintree's
Daughter*, given a
single performance
in 1894.

VICTORIAN ENGLAND

In the England of the late nineteenth century the role of Nora was
the undisputed property of Janet Achurch, who with her husband,
Charles Charrington, had financed the 1889 production. Every
reviewer – even Clement Scott – saw her performance as a rare
theatrical event; what they praised was not so much the way
she tackled specific lines, but the intelligence with which she
approached it. Achurch, who considered the role second only to
that of Lady Macbeth, left the audience free to judge the rights and
wrongs of her action, concerned above all that they appreciate the
realities of her situation (Achurch's comments on the role of Nora
can be read in Michael Egan's *Henrik Ibsen: The Critical Heritage*,
1972, pp. 123–5). Over the years her performance changed its
emphasis, from the childish fun Hennings displayed in the part
to a wild and bitter strength. Her clash with the Helmer of 1897,
Courtenay Thorpe, brought about a powerful curtain appreciated
even by Scott: 'The acting was so good that, if we may express it so,
the man becomes the hysterical woman, and the woman becomes
the silent, sullen, and determined man' (*Daily Telegraph*, 11 May
1897, quoted in *Ibsen's Lively Art: A Performance Study of the
Major Plays* by Frederick J. Marker and Lise-Lone Marker,
1989, p. 59).

LATER PRODUCTIONS

Later productions had to come to terms with the fact that Nora was
no longer their contemporary. While George Bernard Shaw was
premature in rejoicing that women had already been liberated, there
was a widespread sense that Ibsen showed a stuffy and limited
world he himself had helped to make irrelevant. As director Tyrone
Guthrie (1900–71) put it in his 1959 autobiography, audiences no
longer wanted to engage with 'high thinking … in a world of dark
crimson serge tablecloths with chenille bobbles, black horsehair
sofas … and huge, intellectual women in raincoats' (*A Life in the
Theatre*, p. 48). In the 1920s a number of productions used
contemporary dress for *A Doll's House*, with Nora in short skirts
and bobbed hair, but this tended to suggest that she herself was too
timid to take advantage of the freedoms on offer to women.

In 1972 Hans Neuenfels produced the play in Stuttgart as a story about the failure of communication; the characters moved almost like puppets with invisible strings, turning to the audience rather than to one another as if it was a waste of time trying to gain understanding within the marriage – even the children were not addressed directly. The figure of the nurse haunted Nora throughout, softly repeating the word 'duty', like her own emerging consciousness. At the beginning Nora lay on the sofa while Helmer loomed up through a window in the bowler hat of a banker; at the end he lay on the sofa with his arms outstretched as if crucified, while Nora could be seen passing above his head after making her exit.

In 1989 Ingmar Bergman stripped the play of Victoriana and set it in a box lined with red velvet, without doors or windows. Rather than allowing the action to flow, he divided it into fragments. Each was played with an emblematic piece of furniture: at first the tree, surrounded by dolls and toys as if Nora and Helmer inhabited a playpen: then the table, where discussion replaced play; and, lastly, a great brass bed for the final, painful parting. The emphasis was not so much on the liberation of Nora as on the way the characters act as her mirrors; the actors remained on stage throughout, quietly seated on chairs at the side, and stepped forward on cue.

RECENT PRODUCTIONS

One of the most enthusiastically received versions of recent years was Anthony Page's production at the Belasco, New York, in 1997. Janet McTeer played the early Nora in a mannered style which suggested a comic actress beginning to realise her part was unworthy of her, trying out silly voices and gestures to make the best of it. Owen Teale gave her husband real physical authority, with a presence that suggested he could be violent if crossed too often; what made him comic was a brain far slower than his wife's. Between them – as between Krogstad and Mrs Linde – there was a strong sexual bond; this made the final parting agonising, especially as McTeer's Nora struggled to articulate what she had discovered about herself, reborn intellectually even as she was tearing herself away from a relationship that she still craved.

 CHECK THE NET
To see full cast details of this 1997 production, together with dates and information of other Broadway productions, visit the Internet Broadway Database at **www.ibdb.com** and search for 'Doll's House'.

 CHECK THE NET
To read a review of this 1997 production, visit **http://query. nytimes.com** and search for 'The Doll Brings Down the House'.

CONTEXT

E. T. A. Hoffmann's short story 'The Sandman' appeared in 1817 and tells the sinister tale of a man obsessed with a mechanical doll that looks like a real woman but can only say 'Ah, ah!' The ballet *Coppelia, or the Girl with the Enamel Eyes* (1870) gave the story a subversive and feminist comic edge. In an amusingly mechanistic dance style Swanilda takes the doll's place in order to play tricks on both the inventor and her boyfriend, who is smitten with its charms.

In 2000 Polly Teale's production at the New Ambassadors in London with the company Shared Experience, known for its devised work as well as theatre classics, placed a large white doll's house on stage, from which Nora emerged at the beginning, dancing to the sound of a musical box. While both Krogstad and Helmer were played by black actors, Jude Akuwudike and Paterson Joseph respectively, the chilly Norwegian setting was emphasised by the bleached-out colour of everything on stage (and the chunky sweater that Mrs Linde was knitting before Helmer demanded pretty embroidery). Nora's father appeared behind her as a silent ghost, underlining Nora's realisation during her talk with Rank that Helmer was a substitute father rather than a partner. At the end, Anne-Marie Duff's Nora unhooked the wall of the house, as if it were literally a doll's house, and walked into a night of swirling snow.

PART FOUR

CRITICAL PERSPECTIVES

READING CRITICALLY

This section provides a range of critical viewpoints and perspectives on *A Doll's House* and gives a broad overview of key debates, interpretations and theories proposed since the play was published. It is important to bear in mind the variety of interpretations and responses this text has produced, many of them shaped by the critics' own backgrounds and historical contexts.

No single view of the text should be seen as dominant; it is important that you arrive at your own judgements by questioning the perspectives described, and by developing your own critical insights. Objective analysis is a skill achieved through coupling close reading with an informed understanding of the key ideas, related texts and background information relevant to the text. These elements are all crucial in enabling you to assess the interpretations of other readers, and even to view works of criticism as texts in themselves. The ability to read critically will serve you well both in your study of the text, and in any critical writing, presentation or further work you undertake.

> **CONTEXT**
>
> Our word 'critic' comes from the Greek term for the jury who gave the prize for the best play at annual festivals. They were not professionals; they were chosen by lot, because the views of all citizens were considered equally important. This is a useful way of thinking about criticism: it is designed to help you as a fellow reader and theatregoer to form and argue your own views.

RECEPTION AND CRITICAL VIEWS

EARLY CRITICS

Many of the first European responses to *A Doll's House* focused on its ending. The largely Christian and idealist right wavered between expressing desire for a noble and maternal Nora to provide the audience with something to aspire to, and complaining that Ibsen's Nora was unrealistic because women were noble and maternal already. After the Copenhagen premiere the critic and theatre manager M. W. Brun protested in the newspaper *Folkets Avis* that any real wife in Nora's situation would 'throw herself into her husband's arms', and maintained that the 'screaming dissonances' ran counter to common sense (24 December 1879). Writing in the

CHECK THE BOOK

A Beginner's Guide to Critical Reading: Readings for Students by Richard Jacobs (2001) provides entertaining commentary on a range of literary texts. It will help you see how criticism and theory can enhance your own enjoyment and appreciation of literature.

Norwegian paper *Aftenbladet* in January 1880, Fredrik Petersen, a professor of theology at the University of Kristiania, declared that the absence of either a reconciliation scene or the 'uplifted mood' the Greeks imparted to a **tragedy** was a serious flaw: without either the play was 'ugly' and 'distressing' (quoted in Toril Moi's *Henrik Ibsen and the Birth of Modernism: Art, Theater, Philosophy*, 2006, p. 227).

In Germany Ibsen was pressured into writing a happy ending, with Nora, faced by the sight of her children, unable to walk through the door and fainting on the threshold. This was rapidly abandoned, although the journal *Deutsche Rundschau* continued to accuse Ibsen of 'loving the repulsive', while a review in *Die Gegenwart* considered the ending 'illogical and immoral' (quoted in Michael Meyer, *Ibsen*, 1985, p. 482). Such reviews were countered by assertions from the radical and secular left that 'our own life, our own everyday life, has here been placed on stage and condemned!' (quoted in Moi, *Henrik Ibsen and the Birth of Modernism*, 2006, p. 228). But though delighted by the energy of the play, they tended to discuss it only as an attack on marriage; its theatrical complexity and innovation tended to be ignored.

VICTORIAN ENGLAND

By the time the play reached Britain its reputation meant that thousands felt themselves entitled to a view, even if they had not seen or read it. A *Punch* cartoon called 'Ibsen in Brixton' (2 May 1891) shows an enormous grim-faced woman poised at her open front door while two servants stagger out with her luggage. Confronting her cowering shrimp of a husband she proclaims, 'Yes, William, I've thought a deal about it, and I find I'm nothing but your doll and dickey-bird, and so I'm going!' To critique the play was to join a wider debate, for reviews were a forum in which questions about social problems, the status of women and the future of theatre under censorship could be aired. It is not surprising that many who joined the debate were critic-playwrights, like George Bernard Shaw and William Archer, novelists like Henry James, or political activists like Eleanor Marx. Reviews and articles offered the kind of platform a current affairs programme on television might now provide – Shaw considered criticism a form of

QUESTION

Shaw published some of his early drama, influenced by Ibsen, in two volumes called *Plays Pleasant and Unpleasant* (1898). In which category would you put *A Doll's House*, and why?

'gladiatorship' and his role a mixture of 'court jester' and 'confessor' (as described in his preface to the first volume of *Plays Pleasant and Unpleasant*; see p. 9 of the 2000 Penguin edition of *Plays Unpleasant*).

Clement Scott, Ibsen's most implacable enemy in England, centred his attack on the character of Nora; he assumed, without question, that this was inherent rather than formed by her circumstances, demanding: 'How Torvald Helmer could by any possibility have treated his restless, illogical, fractious, and babyish little wife otherwise than he did; why Nora should ever adore with such abandonment and passion this conceited prig … are points that … require a considerable amount of argument … to convince the common-sense playgoer' (*Daily Telegraph*, 8 June 1889; quoted in *Henrik Ibsen: The Critical Heritage*, edited by Michael Egan, 1972, p. 102). The *Spectator* did try to engage with what it termed Ibsen's 'useful lesson' that the infantilising of women leads to 'distorted relations', but castigated him for the 'moral vacuum' at the end, blaming Nora for her unwillingness to 'make a hero where she had failed to find one'. In full-blown idealist vein it warned women to 'beware of confounding the feelings of men who look to them for nothing better than pleasant sensations and mental distractions, with the feelings of men who look to them to raise their ideal of mental and moral grace and beauty' (*Spectator*, 21 June 1889; also quoted in Egan's *Henrik Ibsen*, 1972, pp. 110–13).

One of the most substantial pro-Ibsen manifestos was George Bernard Shaw's *The Quintessence of Ibsenism* (1891), originally a paper to the Fabian Society. What Shaw, like many of his contemporaries in the socialist and suffragist movements, most admired in Ibsen was his 'sharpshooting at the audience … we are not flattered spectators killing the idle hour with an ingenious and amusing entertainment: we are "guilty creatures sitting at a play"' (*The Quintessence of Ibsenism*, 1932 edition, p. 63). Eleanor Marx valued Nora as a woman with complex and adult moral stature; she complained that critical discussion of plays like *A Doll's House* was distorted by a particularly English narrowness which perceived the word 'morality' as 'like the word "virtue" … applied to only one special quality … sexual relations'. Together with Israel Zangwill she wrote a witty **parody** of Ibsen's ending 'to please the critic of

CONTEXT

Scott summarised *Ghosts*, *Hedda Gabler* and *Rosmersholm* thus: 'A few steps out of the hospital ward, and we arrive at the dissecting-room. Down a little lower … and we come to the dead-house. There, for the present, Ibsen has left us' (*Illustrated London News*, 25 April 1891). Scott eventually alienated the whole acting profession by stating that the theatre 'draws out all that is bad in man and woman'.

 CHECK THE NET

You can read this comic parody of the ending of Ibsen's play – 'A Doll's House Repaired' – together with its witty introduction, online; search for 'Eleanor Marx' and 'A Doll's House Repaired' using an online search engine.

the *Daily Telegraph'* in which Helmer realises his wife has been dangerously infected with feminism and packs the children off to boarding school.

LATER CRITICS

By the end of the nineteenth century, however, it was plain that Ibsen, and **naturalism**, would shape much of Western drama and performance. (In 1897 Queen Victoria and the Archbishop of Canterbury went to see *Ghosts*, an odd choice for her Diamond Jubilee treat.) However, Ibsen's work has suffered from a lack of serious reappraisal. This is largely due to the label 'naturalist', which meant that for a long time he was discussed almost exclusively in those terms. By the end of the Second World War naturalism itself was called into question. The influential German critic and philosopher Theodor W. Adorno (1903–69) noted that Ibsen's name called forth boredom, the playwright and his plays both seeming 'outdated' (quoted in Toril Moi's *Henrik Ibsen and the Birth of Modernism: Art, Theater, Philosophy*, 2006, p. 18). For the most thoughtful twentieth-century English critic of Ibsen, the Marxist Raymond Williams, the problem was that 'Ibsen and Stanislavsky have won' (*Drama from Ibsen to Brecht*, 1976, p. 7). He considered that while Ibsen's naturalism had been necessary at the time in order to show the psychological and political limitations of bourgeois domestic life, it was a stage the theatre needed to outgrow. His *Drama from Ibsen to Brecht* locates the future of drama in theatrical techniques that do not disguise their artificiality but embrace it, like the work of Brecht (see **Contemporary approaches: Marxist criticism**).

For others, however, Ibsen is not naturalistic *enough*, the structure of the earlier plays too obvious in comparison with the delicacy of Anton Chekhov (1860–1904). Ronald Gray's *Ibsen: A Dissenting View* (1977) expounds this accusation at length, accusing *A Doll's House* of cynically exploiting the techniques of popular drama. However, to a later generation brought up within some of the newer critical disciplines (see **Contemporary approaches**), the relationship of Ibsen's plays – and *A Doll's House* in particular – to notions of theatricality and performance is precisely what makes them interesting. Toril Moi, in the most radical reappraisal of Ibsen since

---

CONTEXT

Stanislavsky (1863–1938) co-founded the Moscow Art Theatre in 1898 to explore naturalistic technique. The Russian director, actor and teacher maintained that the creativity of the actor must be developed from within, and recorded his own development in *My Life in Art* (1924). The 'method' style of acting derived from his teaching is characterised by spontaneity and improvisation, together with an emphasis on psychological **realism**.

Williams, sees Ibsen as a pioneer of **modernism**. She examines Ibsen's presentation of individuals who simultaneously theatricalise their own experience and see 'theatricality' as an enemy to 'truth' (for more on this idea, see also **Themes: Theatricality**). *A Doll's House*, Moi suggests, is an 'invitation to reflect on the nature of theatre' (*Henrik Ibsen and the Birth of Modernism*, 2006, p. 237). This idea has interesting possibilities for feminist critics (see **Contemporary approaches: Gendered criticism**) and also for performers.

It is not surprising that some of the most interesting recent writers on Ibsen have grounded their studies in performance; for, although critical attention has been lacking, he has never ceased to be one of the most widely produced playwrights. Frederick J. Marker and Lise-Lone Marker, for example, in their work *Ibsen's Lively Art: A Performance Study of the Major Plays* (1989), see the work of designers, directors and actors – especially the interpreters of Nora – as an 'essential dimension' (p. ix) to the understanding of how different generations have understood Ibsen. Egil Törnqvist in *A Doll's House* (1995) explores performances of the play in different media – stage, film and radio – and in both Norwegian and English, in order to highlight the variety of possible interpretations.

**CHECK
THE BOOK**

Moi's *Henrik Ibsen and the Birth of Modernism: Art, Theater, Philosophy* (2006) reappraises Ibsen in the context of literary history and discusses in detail his relationship to the visual arts.

CONTEMPORARY APPROACHES

SIGNS AND SEMIOTICS

Semiotics is the study of signs. The Swiss linguist Ferdinand de Saussure (1857–1913) was the first to define language as a system of words or 'signs' which have no intrinsic relationship to the things they signify but have meanings commonly agreed upon, which distinguish them from other signs for other things (speakers of English, for example, agree that 'cat' means a small furry animal and 'cot' does not). Claude Lévi-Strauss (b.1908) and Roland Barthes (1915–80) expanded this definition to include all kinds of sign systems used to convey meaning between people, such as gestures, clothing and codes of manners. Because these are arbitrary, the relationship between the signifier (the word or image or action) and the signified (the meaning conventionally ascribed to it) can change or slip.

CHECK THE BOOK

Martin Esslin's *The Field of Drama: How the Signs of Drama Create Meaning on Stage and Screen* (1987) is a very useful introduction to theatre semiotics which provides plenty of examples of sign systems at work in well-known plays.

CONTEXT

Brecht maintained that the function of theatre was to transform the world and that the style in which a play was presented was crucial to the process. The *Verfremdungseffekt* or 'alienation effect' required actors to keep a critical distance from their roles, and the action would be broken up with songs, in order that the audience might better appreciate the political forces underlying the **narrative**.

This can be a helpful way to understand a piece of theatre, which is a formal arrangement of different kinds of sign. Names are the most obviously arbitrary labels of all. In *A Doll's House* the word 'Helmer', like any surname, signifies a particular character, but to Nora it has another layer of meaning: she does not use it like most nineteenth-century Norwegian wives, to address her husband, but prefers his first name, 'Torvald'; and this suggests that she perhaps does not perceive him as all a husband should be. Helmer thinks that Krogstad should use his surname not his Christian name, which Helmer considers to signify a friendship between them he does not acknowledge: but when we hear Krogstad speak in Act 2 of 'our worthy Torvald Helmer' (p. 197), his use of the name suggests contempt rather than intimacy.

Physical objects are similarly given a complex weight of signification. The Christmas tree at the beginning indicates the season; it might also signify a set of values to the audience – the Christian ideal of family – or simply festivity and fun. Nora may well link herself to all these at the outset, but towards the end of Act 1 the tree signifies to her – and us – the way she must continually distract her husband by 'dressing' it as she 'dresses' her own worry in a mask of gaiety; its stripped state in the second act is a living image of her exhaustion and vulnerability. Clothing throughout is used in similar ways: Nora's Capri costume sets up tensions between what it immediately signifies: 'the dress of a worker'; its meaning to Helmer: 'a fancy dress showing something about my wife and my power over her'; and Nora's demeanour in Act 3 as she quails in her festive attire as Helmer calls her 'a liar, a hypocrite – even worse – a criminal!' (p. 221). The famous slam of the door which ends the play is also a sign: while its primary meaning is 'Nora has left the building', it is also a comment on the '*glimmer of hope*' with which Helmer ponders the possibility of the 'greatest miracle of all' (p. 232).

MARXIST CRITICISM

A follower of the Marxist playwright Bertolt Brecht (1898–1956) might well attack *A Doll's House* for its **naturalism**. For Brecht, a play that allowed the audience to become absorbed in the action as if they were watching real life was in danger of lulling them into accepting the society shown in the play instead of wanting to change it. He felt that the theatre should constantly call attention to the fact that it *was* theatre, so that the audience could not identify with the sufferings of the **protagonist** but would be alert to the political conditions which caused them, and demand change.

However, a contemporary Marxist critic might view this rather differently. The current preoccupation of Marxist criticism is with what a text does *not* say – because the text itself has been produced on a set of assumptions about the world seen as 'natural' by author and audience alike. The **ideology** of a culture – shared beliefs and values held in an unquestioning manner – is like water to a fish, invisible and unacknowledged. It is not in the interests of the dominant groups in a society to question the way they exclude and marginalise others; consequently they perceive the status quo as an organic growth, rather than a structure for the convenient exercise of power. A Marxist critic might look at a text and ask, 'Whose story does this tell? Is it told at the expense of lower economic groups?' Ibsen's focus on Nora, for example, means that we only see the other women of the Helmer household, the maid and the nurse, in relation to her. The maid's function is to say nothing as she admits suspicious characters like Krogstad, carry letters on bank business and be woken in the middle of the night to present a letter on a tray to Nora. The nurse has her own story, but we have no idea what will happen to her in the new order. Nora goes off to become an individual; we assume from her conversation with Mrs Linde about work that she aspires to become part of the bourgeoisie – the class with sufficient money, leisure and status to afford the luxury of forging a personal identity. But this is to some extent at the expense of the nurse and those of her class who continue to service them.

Both Nora and Mrs Linde themselves, however, have been what a Marxist critic would term **reified** by the society they live in – that is, they have been turned into commodities – and are beginning to articulate the fact. Nora may well have been Helmer's reward for helping her financially embarrassed father, and she describes her marriage as if she were an object, 'pass[ing] out of Papa's hands into yours' (Act 3, p. 226). Although Helmer's nicknames suggestive of household pets make it clear that he sees Nora as a possession, this

CONTEXT

Brecht's legacy lies not only in plays like *Mother Courage* (1941) and *The Caucasian Chalk Circle* (1948) but in the theatre he founded, the Berliner Ensemble, which has influenced performance all over the Western world.

 CHECK THE BOOK

Terry Eagleton's *Literary Theory: An Introduction* (1983) not only explains most current literary and critical perspectives but discusses the conflicts between them.

 CHECK THE BOOK

See Karl Marx and Friedrich Engels's *The Communist Manifesto* (1848) for the ideological basis of much Marxist criticism. It was published just over thirty years before *A Doll's House*.

process of **reification** is not something of which he is consciously aware. Like Nora, Mrs Linde is quite clear in her mind that she has been an object of exchange – she sold herself to a rich husband in order to keep herself and her family. Krogstad expresses bitterness about this fact, but only because he himself suffered as a result; he does not criticise society for allowing such transactions to take place.

Nora, however, does. While she does not discuss her world in explicitly political terms, she does propose to challenge it. She is not yet confident enough to say 'which is right – the law or I' (Act 3, p. 229), but she is no longer an object. She is a subject, who can both learn and speak about what she has learned to others, and the challenge 'Who is right?' is one with which the audience of the play cannot help but engage.

CHECK THE BOOK

Butler's *Gender Trouble: Feminism and the Subversion of Identity* (1990) suggests that 'As in other ritual social dramas, the action of gender requires a performance that is repeated. This repetition is at once a reenactment and a reexperiencing of a set of meanings already socially established' (p. 140). In other words, we regularly perform actions society expects of our gender – childcare for women, warfare for men, for example – and by doing this we also reinforce those expectations.

GENDERED CRITICISM

In 1898 the Norwegian Women's Rights League held a banquet to celebrate Ibsen's seventieth birthday; he made a rather ungracious speech saying that he 'must disclaim the honor of having consciously worked for the women's rights movement' and was interested solely in 'the description of humanity' (quoted in *Ibsen's Women* by Joan Templeton, 2001, p. 110). As Templeton points out in this recent feminist study, this speech has been widely cited by male critics as an excuse to avoid discussing the feminist issues raised by the play. Nevertheless, *A Doll's House* remains one of the most powerful refutations ever written of the theory of separate spheres which underpinned nineteenth-century society – the idea that men and women belonged in the workplace and the home respectively (see **Historical background**). Feminist critics have pointed out that **patriarchal** society has always seen the essential natures of men and women as different, but not as equal. Masculinity has been associated with light, goodness and culture; femininity with darkness, evil and untamed nature – to be fought and defeated.

In contrast, Judith Butler's *Gender Trouble: Feminism and the Subversion of Identity* (1990) suggests that there is no such thing as innate masculinity or femininity. Rather, our gender (as opposed to our biological sex) is performative – that is, gender is not something we *are*, but something we *do*. Society tacitly agrees that certain kinds of behaviour are 'natural': for men, these include working for money, fighting and social control; for women, they involve childbearing, nurturing and submissively pleasing men. Nineteenth-century costumes make this duality apparent. Men dressed plainly, fitting their role as working breadwinners; beards and moustaches stressed their unlikeness to women. ('Torvald' is a Viking name meaning 'thunder power', suggesting a big, strong and hairy male.) The clothes of even moderately well-to-do women were elaborate, emphasising the small waist and large hips that the period considered 'feminine'.

Both Nora and Helmer can be seen determinedly performing their gender stereotypes: we can see her play the submissive and cajoling wife flattering Helmer into giving her friend a job as if she sees work as something for 'frightfully clever' people (Act 1, p. 167). Helmer tells Nora, 'I shouldn't be a proper man if your feminine helplessness didn't make you twice as attractive to me', and offers her the protection of his 'great wings' like some masculine divinity (Act 3, p. 223). Both of them literally dress up in order to express these stereotypes more clearly: Nora as the peasant dancing for Helmer's pleasure, he as the master of the dance in a cloak which suggests his 'great wings'. Both indulge in the language of **melodrama**, a genre which deals in strong heroes and helpless heroines. By the end of the play Nora at least can see these roles as demeaning and corrupting – just as she has ceased to divide people into 'us' and 'strangers'.

CONTEXT

In Scandinavian mythology Thor was the god of thunder, the weather and agriculture. His weapon was a hammer, emblematic of the thunderbolt. (The hammer was also Ibsen's personal symbol, and is carved upon his gravestone.)

PART FIVE

BACKGROUND

CHECK THE BOOK

In 1881 Ibsen wrote a fragment of autobiography about his life in Skien, including a description of the church tower from which a watchman fell to his death after seeing a black dog, an episode that struck his imagination as a child. The fragment is printed in full in Michael Meyer's comprehensive life of the playwright *Ibsen* (1985, pp. 26–31).

CHECK THE NET

Marichen and Knud's first child, Johan Altenburg, died when only eighteen months old, three and a half weeks after Henrik was born. To discover more about Ibsen's family, visit Ibsen.net at **www.ibsen.net** and click on 'Life & Works', 'About Ibsen's Life' and 'Henrik Ibsen's relations and family'.

HENRIK IBSEN'S LIFE AND WORKS

All his life, Henrik Ibsen wrote about money and marriage; and this is not surprising, for both had a devastating effect on his life. His mother, Marichen Altenburg, was the cultured daughter of the richest merchant in Skien, a lumber town on the east coast of Norway; rumour had it that when she married Knud Ibsen, who ran the general store, in 1825 it was a marriage of convenience and that she loved another man. For nine years they lived well and entertained lavishly in the Altenburg family home, producing six children (Henrik Johan was the second, born on 20 March 1828); then Knud lost it all. Everything was sold but one small farmhouse; the family were ostracised and so poor that they often had nothing to eat but potatoes. Knud began drinking heavily and was violent towards Marichen, who became cowed and withdrawn, her only consolations her children and her religion. Ibsen felt the family disgrace keenly; never a sociable child, he paid his schoolfellows to avoid him.

Throughout Ibsen's plays the theme of financial ruin – which provides the mainspring of Nora's story – occurs again and again. Profligate fathers betray their families, like the eccentric old father in *The Wild Duck* (1884) who hangs around the scene of his disgrace in a uniform he is no longer entitled to wear. Nora's father in *A Doll's House* haunts Helmer as an image of all he most fears: the loss of respect as a result of financial irresponsibility. Knud's violence generated an awareness of female powerlessness; though Ibsen drew strong female characters – the bitter Mrs Alving in *Ghosts* (1881), the frustrated Hedda Gabler, Nora emerging from her doll's house into maturity – they lack legal authority to shape their own lives.

While the Ibsens could afford only the most basic education, Marichen was a talented artist and taught her children. Henrik enjoyed inventing plays for dolls he made and painted himself;

he built a spectacular puppet theatre, staging shows people travelled miles to see. University seemed out of the question, so he was apprenticed at sixteen to a pharmacist in Grimstad, a small shipbuilding town a hundred miles away. Too badly paid to afford underclothes, socks or food, at eighteen he had a further demand on his pocket. He had an affair with servant girl Else Jensdatter, who became pregnant, and for fourteen years made support payments to their son, Hans Jacob Henriksen, although he probably never met him. The themes of fatherhood and betrayal (Ibsen wondered about his own paternity) occur in several plays: Hedwig in *The Wild Duck* kills herself when her father rejects her; Oswald in *Ghosts* falls in love with his half-sister; Peer Gynt fathers a child known only as 'Ugly Brat'.

The later Grimstad years marked Ibsen's intellectual flowering; he wrote comic and patriotic verse, drew cartoons, and when the business transferred to a more generous employer he earned enough to move to Kristiania (now Oslo) and work towards university entrance. He made friends, with whom he discussed politics and his emerging atheism; one, Ole Schulerud, admired Ibsen's first play, *Catiline*, and paid for its publication in 1850. Although he never qualified for university Ibsen became a literary force in Kristiania; his poems were widely circulated, and his one-act play *The Warrior's Barrow* was staged in 1850; he found the production 'dreadful' and wrote an essay in the periodical *Manden* demanding 'something new' in Nordic theatre. He was by now terribly in debt, escaping prison by a stroke of luck.

The composer and violinist Ole Bull (1810–80) wanted to develop a distinctively Norwegian culture (Danish was the language of the educated). Bull founded a new theatre at Bergen, Norway's second city, and Ibsen became writer in residence with a mandate to create a new national theatre. He received a grant to visit Copenhagen, where the standard of acting was high – he could recall performances years later – and where he saw his first Shakespeare. He also encountered the work of Eugène Scribe (1791–1861), the prolific writer of formulaic popular drama; despite rating these 'dramatic candy-floss' (quoted in Meyer's *Ibsen*, 1985, p. 93) he bought several scripts, knowing they would be good box office.

CONTEXT

Catiline sold only forty copies of its print run of two hundred and fifty. Ibsen and Schulerud were so poor at this time that they sold the rest to a scrap merchant. 'For the next few days', Ibsen recalled in his preface to the second edition, 'we lacked none of the primary necessities of life' (quoted in Meyer's *Ibsen*, 1985, p. 79) – but they thus made it one of the rarest and most valuable of first editions for collectors.

CONTEXT

Together with friends Paul Botten-Hansen and Aasmund Vinje, Ibsen ran the **satirical** journal *Andhrimner* in 1851; this was informally known as *Manden* (*The Man*). Financial losses forced the magazine to close after less than a year.

He moved to Dresden, where the art gallery captured his imagination and prompted a cycle of poems about art and faith, a theme that features in his later plays.

Back in Bergen, Ibsen found that his shyness made it difficult for him to instruct actors (the idea of a 'director' was in its infancy), but the detailed notebooks where he recorded moves and scenery indicate he was learning stagecraft. The despised Scribe knew how to structure a play, how to relate action to setting and achieve a climax with the fall of each act curtain; the confidence with which Ibsen handles these devices in *A Doll's House* shows he imbibed a great deal of Scribe's technique. The plays written during the six Bergen years he called 'my apprenticeship' (quoted in Robert Ferguson, *Henrik Ibsen: A New Biography*, 1996, p. 65), and fulfilled Bull's instructions to create Norwegian theatre: *St John's Night*, a kind of Norwegian *Midsummer Night's Dream* (written in 1952, but not published until 1909); a revised *Warrior's Barrow*; *The Feast at Solhaug* (1856); *Olaf Liljekrans* (performed in 1857, published in 1902); and, most interesting, *Lady Inger* (first performed in January 1855 and published two years later). Set during the sixteenth-century occupation of Norway by the Danes, *Lady Inger*'s **eponymous** heroine is a resistance fighter torn between patriotism and love for her illegitimate child by a Swedish prince.

One member of the audience who admired *Lady Inger* was Suzannah, nineteen-year-old stepdaughter of Bergen's noted woman writer Magdalene Thoresen. After their second meeting (typically, at a ball where they refused to dance) Ibsen sent Suzannah a poem proposing marriage; when he called to learn her reply, she hid behind the sofa to see how long he would be willing to wait. They married in 1858. By now Ibsen had a new job as artistic director of the Norwegian Theatre in the capital, Kristiania; again, his task was related to national identity – he was in direct competition with Kristiania's grander Danish Theatre. In 1857 Ibsen wrote a nationalist epic, *The Vikings at Helgeland*, naming his son Sigurd after one of the characters, followed by *Love's Comedy* (1862), about a couple who idealistically renounce sex. But the theatre had exceeded its budget; by the time Ibsen wrote his thirteenth-century history play *The Pretenders* in 1863 (it opened

CONTEXT

Bull was one of the greatest violin virtuosos of his time, widely acclaimed for his brilliant improvisations. Born in Bergen, he gave concerts all over Europe and North America, and sought to make the folk music and culture of Norway more widely known. Around 1860 he conceived the idea of a Norwegian Academy of Folk Music, but was unable to gain public sponsorship.

in January 1864) he was on the verge of bankruptcy and fled his creditors to Italy.

The witty and independent Suzannah coped remarkably well with poverty; she discouraged Ibsen's bouts of Knud-like drinking, dissuaded him from abandoning theatre for art and organised a rigid timetable to help his concentration. Fluent in German, French, Italian and English, she passed on to her husband reading matter he found useful. She tolerated his physical timidity: once, thinking Suzannah had contracted the cholera sweeping town, Ibsen refused to fetch the doctor in case he caught the disease himself (it was a false alarm). Suzannah's sharp humour perhaps encouraged Ibsen to find the comedic perspective on cowardice which emerges in the **ironic** treatment of Torvald Helmer in *A Doll's House*.

Within four years, Ibsen's fortunes altered. His verse play *Brand* was published in 1866 with immediate commercial and critical success. Although he considered it anti-Norwegian (he was disgusted by his country's refusal to help the Danes in their struggle with Germany for Schleswig-Holstein), *Brand*'s powerful story is supported by dazzling images of the Norwegian landscape. Brand is a priest who sacrifices mother, wife and child to the principle 'All or nothing' (Act 3), dying in an avalanche as a mysterious voice cries, 'He is the God of love' (Act 5). Although radically different from *A Doll's House*, one of *Brand*'s central conflicts is between a man standing for absolute ideals and a woman believing like Nora that love comes first; it is crystallised in an image of the woman talking to the man through a closed door, a stage picture comically reprised by Nora and Helmer.

Brand led to a lifetime grant from the Norwegian government. Ibsen summered in Sorrento and began a play exploring everything *Brand* was not. *Peer Gynt*, written so quickly it was published only a year later (although its first performance was not until 24 February 1876), is a sprawling epic rich in comedy; it draws on Norwegian folklore to create a work-shy, faithless anti-hero who gets mixed up with trolls, seduces women, becomes a capitalist with an interest in steamships and finally realises that he is like an onion, with nothing at its heart. The motto 'To thyself be enough', which

CONTEXT

Ibsen wrote a series of love poems to Suzannah addressing her as 'Cat'. These were destroyed at his death, but he published one, 'Thanks' (in Norwegian, *tak*, which is 'kat' spelled backwards). One verse expresses her feminist spirit: 'Her home lies here / On Freedom's sea / Where the poet's ship / Finds its mirror.' The poem is quoted in full in Meyer's *Ibsen* (1985, p. 351).

CONTEXT

The *Peer Gynt*
Suite by Edvard
Grieg (1843–1907)
was an immediate
success and
remains one of
the most popular
and accessible
selections of
classical music. It
was Ibsen's idea
that he and Grieg
should collaborate,
but Ibsen disliked
the music and
dismissed a
producer, August
Lindberg, who
subsequently
suggested the two
of them should
work on *Brand*
because of the
success of the *Gynt*
suite, snapping,
'So you think that's
good, do you?'

**CHECK
THE BOOK**

For more
information on the
Saxe-Meiningen
Company, see
Chapter 3
(pp. 11–17) of
J. L. Styan's *Modern
Drama in Theory
and Practice:
Realism and
Naturalism* (1981).

the trolls teach the wily Peer, poses the same question as *Brand*:
how does the individual balance the responsibility to develop the
self with responsibility to the wider world? This would be Nora's
dilemma, just a few years later.

Peer Gynt's success brought further grant money, and the family
moved to Dresden. Ibsen made trips to Sweden and Egypt, but
did not return home on the death of his mother in 1869, writing
defensively to his favourite sister: 'don't think I am lacking in
warmth' (quoted in Robert Ferguson, *Henrik Ibsen: A New
Biography*, 1996, p. 146). Norway was on his mind, however, and
his 1869 prose **comedy** about Norwegian politics, *The League of
Youth* – after a rough reception by members of the audience who
recognised some of the public figures it lampooned – became one
of the most popular plays of the century in Norway.

For some years Ibsen wrestled with a trilogy inspired by his stay
in Rome, which became the double play *Emperor and Galilean*.
The story of Emperor Julian's relationship with Christianity and
paganism, it reflected his own rejection of the faith to which his
mother and sisters clung. The play has only been staged once in its
entirety (it runs at eight hours), but sold in great numbers when
published in 1873 and marked a personal watershed for Ibsen. In
1874 he made a brief return trip to Norway, where the Kristiania
Theatre staged *The League of Youth* and students feted him with
a torchlight procession; movingly, he likened himself to Julian,
valued by sensible people but not close to their hearts, and said
the warmth of their reception was his 'richest prize' (quoted in
Ferguson, *Henrik Ibsen*, 1996, p. 187). He avoided Skien and the
family, however, and soon returned to Germany. In Berlin in 1876
he encountered the Saxe-Meiningen production of *The Pretenders*.
The company's ensemble acting, **realistic** scenery and sophisticated
lighting were a revelation; Ibsen wrote a long-planned **naturalistic**
play, the instantly acclaimed *Pillars of Society*, about hypocrisy and
corruption in a town like Grimstad. This was published in 1877,
and in the same year, the University of Uppsala awarded him a
doctorate to celebrate its four hundredth anniversary; for the rest
of his life he called himself 'Dr Ibsen', and felt the family disgrace
was redeemed. His father died that year; Ibsen did not go home,

but sent a photograph of himself, posted the day *The Pillars of Society* opened in Copenhagen.

The idea for *A Doll's House* may well have been germinating during Ibsen's long struggle with *Emperor and Galilean*. Ibsen's friend Brandes had admired the character of Selma in *The League of Youth*, who complains: 'You dressed me up like a doll. You played with me the way one plays with a child' (Act 3), suggesting that she was worthy of a play to herself. Then in 1878 Ibsen received a letter from a friend, Laura Kieler (1849–1932), whose novel *Brand's Daughters* – written as a sequel to *Brand* under her maiden name Petersen when she was just nineteen – had interested him some years previously. Like Torvald Helmer, Kieler's husband had been seriously ill, leading her to contract secret debts for a southern holiday. She asked Ibsen's help in publishing her new novel, *Ultima Thule*, in order to meet the payments. Ibsen refused, saying it was poorly written, and encouraged her to tell her husband about the debt. In October that same year he heard the end of the story: Laura Kieler forged a bank draft; the strain drove her to a breakdown and she was sent to an asylum from which she was discharged into her husband's care. Eleven days later, Ibsen began his notes towards the 'Tragedy of Modern Times' that became *A Doll's House*.

The resulting controversy did no harm to Ibsen's pocket: he described 1880, year of the Munich production, as a 'bumper year' (quoted in Ferguson, *Henrik Ibsen*, 1996, p. 248). The new confidence he acquired after the Saxe-Meiningen experience is reflected in the intense detail in his stage directions and the new close focus on private relationships. From homes in Italy and Germany he wrote *Ghosts* (1881), *An Enemy of the People* (1882), *The Wild Duck* (1884), *Rosmersholm* (1886), *The Lady from the Sea* (1888) and *Hedda Gabler* (1890). Ibsen's biographer Robert Ferguson likens these to the religious group which attracted Marichen in Skien, the Lammers Movement. They forbade the use of curtains, thus opening up the domestic interior to public scrutiny. Ibsen showed people in ordinary houses, their often tragic lives shaped by heredity or pressure from the past, like the diseased Oswald in *Ghosts* and the dying Dr Rank in *A Doll's House*; by their sexuality, like Hedda Gabler and Rebecca West in

CHECK THE BOOK

In the summer of 1871 Laura visited Dresden and met Ibsen; he called her his 'skylark'. Later she married a Danish schoolteacher, Victor Kieler. Joan Templeton in her work *Ibsen's Women* (2001) gives a detailed account of this episode (pp. 135–7).

CONTEXT

Ghosts would have been highly topical in an England where women had launched the social purity movement of the 1890s. The heart of the movement was grounded in a concern about the growing incidence of syphilis in wives who were infected by straying husbands. The government's only attempt to address this issue had been the notorious 1864 Contagious Diseases Act, which treated women themselves as the source of the problem.

CHECK THE NET

Robins's *Ibsen and the Actress* (1928) is a touching record of Ibsen's impact on her artistic and political life. Her own play, *Votes for Women* (1907), shows a young woman learning about suffrage issues while discovering that her MP fiancé has personally betrayed the vital and dynamic suffragist Vida Levering. You can find a website with details of this prolific actress, playwright and novelist, including a link to the electronic text of *Votes for Women*, at **www.jsu.edu** – search for 'Elizabeth Robins web home page'.

CONTEXT

Sigurd married Bergliot, the youngest daughter of Ibsen's old friend and rival Bjørnstjerne Bjørnson, in 1892. Their first child, Tancred, was born a year later.

Rosmersholm; by an idealism that insists on uncovering truth at any price, like Gregers Werle in *The Wild Duck*, who causes death and disaster by demanding that Hedwig's paternity be revealed.

While controversy raged – every country in which Ibsen plays had been staged initially rejected *Ghosts*, even when they had finally permitted the original ending of *A Doll's House* – Ibsen was financially secure. Printed texts sold well and he was astute enough to ensure publication just before Christmas as often as possible (*Ghosts* must be the unlikeliest stocking filler of all time). He also gained the support of William Archer (1856–1924), who came in search of him in Rome in time to read the final draft of *Ghosts*; he considered it a 'bombshell' (quoted in Ferguson, *Henrik Ibsen*, 1996, p. 271). Archer's six-month stay bore fruit: he became the most distinguished British translator of Ibsen of his day, and his passionate advocacy ensured that by the time Ibsen wrote *Hedda Gabler* the English theatre no longer had to wait years to see it. Elizabeth Robins played Hedda at the Vaudeville Theatre in April 1891 and was cheered enthusiastically, while the ever-reliable Clement Scott continued to attract audiences with references to 'wicked women, deceitful friends, sensualist egotists, piled up in a heap … a hideous play!' (quoted in Ferguson, *Henrik Ibsen*, 1996, p. 355).

Ibsen saw productions of his work throughout Europe – occasionally becoming peevish when labelled a 'socialist' or when German writers expressed resentment at the pre-eminence of a Norwegian in their theatre. But in 1891 Suzannah, missing friends and family, persuaded him to go home. Ibsen sailed round the North Cape of Norway, tossing a wreath of roses into the Arctic. He could be wintry at official receptions in his honour, even snubbing his friend and ally Brandes; he preferred the company of young women, which Suzannah tolerated with her usual good nature, although when Sigurd married she found it a strain being alone with her husband. He also met Laura Kieler again – an awkward encounter. Socially conservative to the point of attacking radical artists in her own work, Kieler resented the way she was perceived by her community as 'the real Nora'.

Rapidly, Ibsen's Norwegian days became as regimented as those in Rome or Dresden – regular periods of work and regular walks to the same café, where he sat at the same table, something of a tourist attraction. His work remained 'naturalistic' in the sense of recognisable, contemporary settings and restrained, non-declamatory language, but next to the domestic details that enliven the earlier plays – Nora's macaroons, Aunt Juju's battered old hat on which Hedda Gabler focuses her contempt for family life – there is a new simplicity and poetry. Characters are taken from folklore, like the Rat Wife in *Little Eyolf* (1894) who taunts a pair of guilty lovers and steals the crippled child who is the token of their remorse: it is as if the world of Helmer has been invaded by Peer Gynt. *John Gabriel Borkman* (1896) repeats the theme of bankruptcy, but the hero dies in a forest clearing where he can sense 'veins of iron ore' reaching out to him (Act 4). At the end of his final play, *When We Dead Awaken* (1899), a sculptor and his model live out for the last time the conflict between duty to the artist-self and duty to love; they die in an avalanche as a nun reaches out her hand to bless them in a clear echo of *Brand*. Ibsen was tiring, and he wanted his work to come full circle. If he wrote again, he noted in the newspaper *Verdens Gang* in 1899, the theatre might no longer be adequate for what he wanted to express: 'If I write anything more, it will be in quite another context; perhaps, too, in a another form' (quoted in Meyer, *Ibsen*, 1985, p. 829).

He did not. But the play was staged in January 1900 at the new, purpose-built National Theatre in Kristiania; Ibsen had truly come home. It was also staged by companies all over Europe – including the Moscow Art Theatre, co-founded by Stanislavsky in 1898, the first to articulate a theory of naturalistic acting which was partly grounded in his experience of acting Ibsen. Not everyone responded favourably to the play (Archer hated it), but one person who did was the young James Joyce (1882–1941), who changed the novel as Ibsen had changed the theatre. Two months later Ibsen had a slight stroke. He recovered, and in November, in an interview for the newspaper *Ørebladet*, spoke about the Boer War, expressing contempt not just for British treatment of the Boers but for the Boers' treatment of the Africans. It was his last public appearance. A second stroke followed in the summer of 1901, and a third in

CONTEXT

The expatriate Irish writer James Joyce is famed for his radically new treatment of human consciousness. He is best known for his novel *Ulysses* (1922) and its highly controversial successor *Finnegans Wake* (1939), as well as the short-story collection *Dubliners* (1914) and the autobiographical *A Portrait of the Artist as a Young Man* (1914–15). A good linguist, in 1901 Joyce wrote an admiring letter in Dano-Norwegian to Ibsen.

1903. He lived on quietly, cared for by Suzannah and his daughter-in-law, Bergliot, until 23 May 1906. His last word, fittingly enough, was *'Tvertimod'* – 'On the contrary' (quoted in Ferguson, *Henrik Ibsen*, 1996, p. 433).

CHECK THE POEM

While Ibsen was often at odds with his country, he wrote a long epic poem, *Terje Vigen*, traditional in form and language, which was published in 1862. It instantly achieved popular success, and until recently every Norwegian schoolchild knew it by heart. It tells of a poor sailor whose family die of starvation when he is captured by a cruel English lord; years later he holds the lord's life in his hands and shows him mercy.

CONTEXT

Landsmaal (known as *nynorsk* since 1929) was adopted as an official language in Norway in 1885. Before the advent of *landsmaal* the formal language used for writing was *riksmaal*, based on the Danish language.

HISTORICAL BACKGROUND

NEW NORWAY

Ibsen was born into a time of change. As the Napoleonic Wars were coming to an end, fourteen years before his birth, the Danish king had ceded Norway to Karl XIV of Sweden; but within this union the Norwegians had rapidly acquired a liberal constitution and a degree of independence, with their own parliament, the Storting, and their own capital, Kristiania. Throughout Ibsen's lifetime the struggle to retain this independence continued, although it was only achieved in 1905, a year before his death.

It was patriotic enthusiasm for specifically Norwegian culture that underlay Ole Bull's mandate to Ibsen to create a Norwegian national theatre. Danish was still the language of the cultured and the language of drama, as no classical plays had yet been translated into *landsmaal*. *Landsmaal* had been developed by the philologist Ivar Aasen (1813–96) to formalise distinctively Norwegian rhythms and pronunciations into a written language subtly different from Danish or Swedish. It allowed the sounds of the Old Norse sagas and the speech rhythms of the peasantry to colour the literature of Norway for the first time. (To understand the limitations the old written forms had placed on Norwegian writers, it may help to imagine Ibsen's contemporary Emily Brontë trying to write *Wuthering Heights* without using the distinctive vocabulary of her native Yorkshire.) At the time of Ibsen's birth, about ninety per cent of the population of one million were involved in agriculture and their way of life was not very different from that of the Middle Ages. By the time he was writing *A Doll's House*, the economy was capitalist and industrialised, the scattered towns linked by railways and the telegraph, and the population had doubled in size despite mass emigration to America. While power still lay in the hands of the judiciary, the intellectuals and the armed forces, there were new social groups: an industrial working class, largely powerless; an expanding middle class; and a more socially mobile petite bourgeoisie of lawyers and officials (to which Helmer clearly belongs, and to which Krogstad aspires).

The year 1848 was one of revolutions in Europe and brought a radical reform movement to Norway led by Marcus Thrane, which defended the rights of poor farmers and factory workers. This was brutally put down with the aid of the Swedish monarchy, and the farming population found itself bitterly divided over the issue. Ibsen felt considerable sympathy for the Thranist cause, although he lacked the courage for direct action. His early comedy *The League of Youth* (1869) reflects his sense of the ubiquity of political corruption and incompetence. The narrowness of Norwegian nationalism increasingly exasperated him. In 1863 the death of Frederik VII of Denmark opened up the question of German rights to the duchies of Schleswig and Holstein; by February 1864 Otto von Bismarck had invaded Schleswig. Karl XV of Sweden and Norway at once offered Denmark his support, only to find that the Storting tied his hands. By April the Prussian army had stormed the Danish town of Dybbol and Ibsen was watching Danish cannon paraded in triumph through Berlin. He never forgave his country for the betrayal of its fellow Scandinavians.

By 1882 the Norwegian left had won a significant election victory, but did little with its power; Liberals and Conservatives alternated in the following decades without much interest in social change and the process of extending the franchise was slow. *An Enemy of the People* (1882) shows one man's struggle against the bureaucratic complacency of a town that draws its income from a dangerously infected public bath. He cries: 'The majority is never right.' Ibsen, smarting from his country's rejection of *Ghosts* (1881), was cynical about the ability of committees to make any kind of rational decisions, but – as he noted more coolly in his notes towards *The Wild Duck* (1884) – 'those qualified to vote are only a small and arbitrarily limited minority' (Edvard Beyer, *Ibsen: The Man and His Work*, 1978, p. 136). *Rosmersholm*, written after his trip to Norway in 1885, explores the implications of the parliamentary system established the previous year, and in particular its

CHECK THE FILM
In 1916 *Terje Vigen* was filmed by the actor-director Victor Sjöström (1879–1960), famous for his beautiful treatment of the Scandinavian landscape. Not only does the brilliant photography help to convey a sense of the quality of Ibsen's poetic language to a non-native speaker, it provides a visual impression of a Norway not very different from the one Ibsen knew.

CHECK THE NET
For more information about the politics and history of Norway during the nineteenth century, go to **www.norway. org.uk**

relationship to freedom of speech and conscience. Its hero breaks with the conservatives and works for a 'true democracy' which would make 'all my countrymen noblemen'.

NEW SCIENCE

CONTEXT

From 1826 onwards Louis Daguerre (1789–1851), partly in conjunction with Joseph Niépce, perfected his daguerreotype process.

If Ibsen had been born into a rich family, he might have been one of the first people to have a photograph of themselves as a baby, the earliest recorded photographs having been produced on metal plate the previous year. The art of photography continued to develop throughout his lifetime; families like the Helmers were certainly in a position to sit for a daguerreotype of themselves, and by the time he had written *Hedda Gabler* in 1890 the first Kodaks had appeared. Photography fascinated Ibsen. It meant that ordinary people could record and interpret portraits of one another, a right once restricted to those rich enough to commission paintings. The discipline for which Ibsen's son Sigurd developed a growing passion, sociology, had also begun to establish itself: since the 1850s Eilert Sundt had been carrying out surveys and demographic studies of the Norwegian people. Suddenly the middle class was interested in itself, and it was only logical that the theatre should show Noras and Helmers rather than the **tragedies** of kings and queens. Psychiatry was still in its infancy; Sigmund Freud was born twenty-eight years after Ibsen and did not begin research into mental disorders until 1885, but it is no surprise that he was an admirer of Ibsen. Freud's concern with the way that close attention to everyday language can reveal **motivation** – through jokes, dreams, the choice of **metaphors** and slips of the tongue – made sense to a world in which Ibsen had begun the move towards a **naturalistic** theatre concerned to explore and record such things with all the accuracy at its disposal.

CHECK THE BOOK

In Act 5 Scene 10 of *Peer Gynt* the sinister Thin Person uses Daguerre's technique of printing from negatives using silver salts as a metaphor for the making of a better self: 'I develop it. / I steam it and dip it, I burn it and cleanse it / With sulphur and similar ingredients, / Till the picture appears which the plate was intended to give. / (I mean, the one known as the positive.)' (*Plays: Six*, translated by Michael Meyer, p. 175.)

This was also the world of Charles Darwin. In 1859 he published *On the Origin of Species by Means of Natural Selection*. Rooted in close observation of the natural world, it suggested that some species – including the human race – had survived and developed by adapting themselves to existing conditions while others vanished because they were less 'fit' to do so. This undermined the literal interpretation of the Genesis account of the Creation; for those who, like Ibsen, already struggled with the religious certainties with which they had grown up, it meant that society had to devise moral codes for itself. *A Doll's House* (1879) and *Ghosts* (1881) explored the questions of heredity, survival and the struggle of the individual towards meaning in a life without religion just as new Danish translations of Darwin had been published. This would not have surprised Émile Zola, who considered naturalism in art the proper response to the blossoming of new sciences: 'today they are still very young, but they are growing and leading us to truth in a movement that is sometimes disturbing because of its rapidity. It is enough to mention cosmology and geology, which have struck such a terrible blow at the fables of religion' ('Naturalism in the Theatre', in *Documents of Modern Literary Realism*, edited by George J. Becker, 1963, p. 200). Nora's determination to think for herself rather than accept what the Church has taught her, and Helmer's shock at the very idea, would have found echoes all over Scandinavia.

NEW WOMEN

Ibsen's reservations about liberty under the emerging parliament led him to believe that 'a new nobility' would have to enter the administration. 'I am obviously not thinking of a nobility of birth … I am thinking of one of character, a nobility of mind and will,' he wrote (quoted in Edvard Beyer, *Ibsen: The Man and His Work*, 1978, p. 146), and prophesied that this would come from the working class and from women. The shift in Norway from agriculture to manufacturing had had a profound effect on women and the family. Men and women on the farms had worked in separate groups with whom they identified strongly, and this spilled over into cultural life: in churches, for example, the sexes once sat apart and made their responses as representatives of their whole gender. Industrialisation, which relied on every single worker concentrating on a monotonous task with its pace set by a machine rather than a group of people, led to a focus on individual rather than group identity. Now men and women sat in church as married couples and responded as part of a family unit rather than a wider group.

As the home ceased to be the basis of cottage industry, there was a greater desire for privacy and individual space within it and this led to a slightly more formal relationship between men and women. In his youth, Ibsen would have known many women like Peer Gynt's

CHECK THE BOOK
Matthew Kneale's modern novel *English Passengers* (2000), set in the mid nineteenth century, describes an expedition to find the true site of the Garden of Eden, led by a vicar who seeks to disprove the 'Atheism' of modern geology (see pp. x, 18–19).

CHECK THE BOOK
Zola's novel of murder and adultery in a lower-middle-class setting, *Thérèse Raquin* (1867), was an early milestone of naturalism; and the preface to the second edition (1868) spells out his ideas on the subject. Ibsen disliked being compared with Zola (see J. L. Styan's *Modern Drama in Theory and Practice: Realism and Naturalism*, 1981, pp. 10–11).

mother, Aase, knowing little of the world outside her own hut and scratching a living from the soil; by the time he had reached middle age, white-collar women like Mrs Linde were common. Norwegian women entered education in 1876, when the first woman was given the right to sit the secondary school examination, and by 1882 they had the right to go to university. For families as poor as Ibsen's had been, however, it was almost impossible for these rights to be used, and working women, whether factory hands, teachers or office workers, earned far less than men, had little prestige and, in the case of the middle class, had to give up work if they chose to marry. As with the petite bourgeoisie right across Europe, a man's social status was enhanced by a wife who remained in the home. Although Helmer treats the extravagance of his 'skylark' as a problem, he would be shocked to know that she can earn money; like most men of his time he believes in the idea of separate spheres – that the sexes are spiritually and biologically designed to operate in separate worlds, the male engaged in the cut and thrust of work and the woman remaining in the home.

Throughout Europe agitation for the rights of women had long been part of the fabric of revolution. Flora Tristan (1803–44), for example, encountered some of the problems faced by Ibsen's own characters: she was denied her inheritance after being declared illegitimate, and when she divorced her abusive husband she lost custody of her children. Campaigning for the rights of the working class in France, she declared that socialism and feminism were inextricably linked. Mary Wollstonecraft published *A Vindication of the Rights of Women* in 1792 – just three years after the start of the French Revolution, and three years after the march on Versailles by thousands of women determined to force both the king *and* the National Assembly to address the matter of providing the people with bread. Wollstonecraft gave a remarkably precise analysis of the real harm in Helmer's 'separate spheres' approach: that women were morally infantilised by it, educated to 'be pleasing at the expense of every solid virtue' (quoted in Joan Templeton, *Ibsen's Women*, 2001, p. 120).

Ibsen's close friend Camilla Collett (1813–95) was profoundly influenced by the feminist novelist George Sand (1804–76);

CHECK THE POEM

Alfred Tennyson's poem *The Princess* (1847) describes the idea of separate spheres in terms the would-be heroic Helmer would no doubt admire: 'Man for the sword and for the needle She'.

CONTEXT

Flora Tristan, travelling through France, recorded this remark from a printer on the subject of equal pay for women: 'We pay them less and that's very fair because they are quicker than men. They would earn too much if we paid them at the same rate' (*L'Union ouvrière*, 1843).

Collett saw her novel *The District Governor's Daughters* (published in two parts in 1854 and 1855) as 'the first swallow' of Norwegian feminism. Her essay *From the Camp of the Dumb* (1877) accused the major writers of the last century – from the French Romantics to the English Victorians – of being unable to imagine a woman who was not 'Half teasing demon, half saint … fire in a crust of ice, or the other way around' (quoted in Templeton, *Ibsen's Women*, 2001, p. 69). Ibsen notoriously denied any form of literary influence, but he admired Collett enough to include a semi-quotation from her novel in *Love's Comedy* (1862). When he began, like Collett, to write about contemporary bourgeois life, his heroines changed. In his historical dramas they are strong, articulate and often wield significant power. In his plays of modern life they are marginalised, considered by their menfolk to be unfit to run their own lives and subject to petty conventions.

Nora is perhaps the first of Ibsen's characters to be fully aware that she is at odds with her society, and it is small wonder that the play found both eager audiences and conservative critics all over Europe and America. Socialist feminists like Eleanor Marx (1855–98) embraced the possibility of debate on what was known as 'the Woman Question'. The *Doll's House* controversy provided it with a focus. Anxiety about gender roles was acute in nineteenth-century England. During Ibsen's lifetime Parliament passed new legislation about divorce, the age of consent, venereal disease and homosexuality. The women's suffrage movement in the UK was concerned with many aspects of women's lives besides the question of the vote. Prompted by the government's Helmer-like reasons for withholding the franchise – Elizabeth Robins noted that she had been herself conditioned to believe in 'woman's limitations, her well-known inability to stick to the point, her poverty in logic and in humour' (quoted in Sheila Stowell's *A Stage of Their Own: Feminist Playwrights of the Suffrage Era*, 1992, p. 11) – they adopted the motto 'Let justice be done though the heavens fall.'

The Actresses' Franchise League, formed in 1908, two years after Ibsen's death, involved most of the women in the profession. They supported all groups seeking female suffrage, but especially the Women's Social and Political Union with its policy of direct and

---

CONTEXT

The term 'New Woman' was used to describe late nineteenth-century writings tackling issues of social change. These included the desire for better educational and employment opportunities for women. New Woman authors also attacked sexual double standards, and questioned the traditional attitudes towards marriage and motherhood.

CONTEXT

The Actresses' Franchise League staged suffrage events and readings, and members wrote and produced plays to support the cause. Members included Elizabeth Robins, Ellen Terry and Sybil Thorndike. By 1914 there were nine hundred members, and branches in all major British cities.

CHECK THE BOOK

Dickens's *David Copperfield* (1849–50) explores the marriage of the hero to Dora, his 'child-wife'. David struggles as Dora fails to grow up and make the marriage an equal partnership, but Dickens evades the long-term implications by letting her die young, thereby freeing David to marry the sensible Agnes. The dying Dora tells him: 'I am afraid it would have been better, if we had only loved each other as a boy and girl, and forgotten it' (Chapter 53).

CHECK THE BOOK

Dostoevsky's *Crime and Punishment* is the story of a student who commits murder. After being pursued by a relentless detective he finally admits responsibility and is sent to a prison camp, where he finds redemption with the help of a saintly young woman.

dramatic action. Many of its more committed members felt that they owed their political education to Ibsen; certainly he had offered the most persuasive and convincing language for society to debate an assertion that Karl Marx had made thirty-five years before Nora slammed the front door: 'The most direct, natural and necessary relation of person to person is the relation of man to woman … from this relationship one can therefore judge man's whole level of development' (*Economic and Philosophical Manuscripts*, 1844).

LITERARY AND THEATRICAL BACKGROUND

GENERAL INFLUENCES: DRAMA AND PROSE

Ibsen once told the Swedish artist Georg Pauli (1855–1935): 'I don't read books, I leave them to my wife and Sigurd' (quoted in Michael Meyer, *Ibsen*, 1985, p. 500). This was disingenuous. During his apprenticeship at the pharmacy he devoured many books which he had brought from Skien, including quantities of Charles Dickens (1812–70). Later he expressed deep respect for the emerging **realist** novelists of Russia, particularly Leo Tolstoy (despite the fact that Tolstoy loathed him). Perhaps because its theme of personal responsibility and guilt preoccupied him in his own plays, Ibsen named *Crime and Punishment* (1866) as the Russian work he most admired; he lived in Dresden at the same time as Fyodor Dostoevsky (1821–81), although they never met. However, Ibsen could be sly about his acquaintance with major authors that others might assume he knew well: he told Archer in 1882, for example, that he had not read Émile Zola; but in 1898 he assured a journalist that he had read a great deal; this may reflect the fact that he had by then brushed up his Zola, but he never seemed to have difficulty in disparaging Zola's work during that whole decade. Largely self-taught, Ibsen probably liked to keep those lucky enough to have an expensive education guessing. But he must also have been aware of just how innovative his own work was.

This makes it difficult to speak with assurance on Ibsen's *specific* influences. However, Georg Brandes memorably observed that Ibsen had a preternatural awareness of the issues that would become important, with an acute ear for 'the low rumble that tells of ideas undermining the ground' (quoted in Meyer, *Ibsen*, 1985, p. 500). This sprang from the fact that he was a passionate reader of newspapers; he also profited from conversation with the well-read Suzannah, listening to her views on writers he could not read in their original languages, and, of course, from his friendship with Brandes himself.

It is not difficult to trace the concerns Ibsen shared with the major novelists of the nineteenth century. There was in all the realists or **naturalists** a forceful rejection of the idealism that characterised late eighteenth-century art and literature. This can best be defined as the belief that art leads us towards human perfectibility; it offers a vision of truth and beauty, a vision of Utopia. Friedrich von Schiller (1759–1805), the greatest playwright of what became known as *Sturm und Drang* ('storm and stress') verse and plays, proclaimed in his 1795–6 manifesto *Über naive und sentimentalische Dichtung* (*On Simple and Sentimental Poetry*) that 'the portrayal of the ideal is what makes the poet' (quoted in Toril Moi, *Henrik Ibsen and the Birth of Modernism: Art, Theater, Philosophy*, 2006, p. 75). Idealism at the height of the **Romantic movement** had given rise to powerfully moving art which, imbued with the idea that humans are naturally good, was often politically radical.

However, as the nineteenth century progressed, the energies that drove this heightened idealism began to wane; while the least attractive quality of the idealists – the tendency to portray women only as saints or devils – still pervaded popular literature, 'sentimental' now meant not 'ennobling' but 'full of cheap emotion'. Reacting against this simplistic approach, the modern novel began to explore in depth the interaction between characters and the realities of their environment – whether driven by the biological imperative to survive, as examined by Darwin (see **Historical background: New science**), or the realities of the class struggle as dissected by Marx. Their scope might encompass a small town, like George Eliot's *Middlemarch* (1871–2); a world convulsed by war, like Tolstoy's *War and Peace* (1865–9); or an adulterous marriage, like Gustave Flaubert's *Madame Bovary* (1857) – but in all cases the story was driven by the interaction of the characters

> **CONTEXT**
>
> The work of Schiller is well represented by the stormy *Die Räuber* (1781, *The Robbers*), written when he was still at school. It dramatises the conflict between two brothers: the elder leads a group of rebellious students into the Bohemian forest to become bandits; the younger schemes to inherit the family estate. The play's treatment of social corruption and its republican ideals made Schiller an overnight sensation. Later Schiller was made an honorary member of the French Republic for the impact of *Die Räuber*.

 CHECK THE BOOK

The Oxford Companion to English Literature, edited by Margaret Drabble (revised sixth edition, 2006), has a useful essay on Romanticism.

with their social, economic and material circumstances. The author declined to offer moral judgements on the characters but coolly displayed them in all their frailty with what Flaubert called 'the precision of the physical sciences ... a pitiless method' (*Documents of Modern Literary Realism*, edited by George J. Becker, 1963, p. 95).

Ibsen had already expressed a desire for drama that did not tie up the ends neatly at the fall of the curtain but where 'the true end lies beyond ... it is now up to each one of us to find his or her own way there' (quoted in Meyer, *Ibsen*, 1985, p. 162). However, the lack of good translations meant that there were no European playwrights on whom he could confidently model himself; he had to define what he wanted by rejecting what he did *not* like about the 'candy-floss' comprising most of the repertoire. His conclusions were not very different from those of Émile Zola in the essay 'Naturalism in the Theatre' (1880). Zola claimed that the forceful intensity of the past had been simply a 'clearing of the ground ... only a superb affirmation of the nothingness of the rules and of the need for life' (*Documents of Modern Literary Realism*, edited by Becker, 1963, p. 211). Turning to the contemporary playwrights of his own country, Zola accused them of being in thrall to the **well-made play**. Eugène Scribe's formula for drama – **exposition, development and complication**, crisis and **resolution**, developed for maximum **suspense** across three or four acts, each ending with an exciting curtain – had once provided a useful framework for containing the passions of idealist drama, but now it inhibited the new generation of playwrights and made their work formulaic. Zola proclaimed a need to 'clear the way' for someone to transform the theatre (*Documents of Modern Literary Realism*, edited by Becker, 1963, p. 219).

Ibsen was pleased with *The League of Youth* (1869), his first play about what he called the 'forces and frictions of modern life' (quoted in J. L. Styan's *Modern Drama in Theory and Practice: Realism and Naturalism*, 1981, p. 18), and boasted that he had managed it 'without a single monologue or aside' (quoted in Meyer, *Ibsen*, 1985, p. 311) – standard Scribean devices – but he hardly behaved like a man about to fulfil Zola's demands by

> **CONTEXT**
>
> Danish critic and scholar Georg Brandes (1842–1927) delivered a series of lectures at the University of Copenhagen over the course of twelve years. Starting on 3 November 1871, these lectures were published later as *Main Currents in Nineteenth Century Literature* in six volumes between 1872 and 1890.

embarking on his massive history play *Emperor and Galilean*. In the course of writing it, however, Ibsen met Georg Brandes. Brandes disagreed with Ibsen on many issues but his *Main Currents in Nineteenth Century Literature* insisted that Scandinavian writers must confront contemporary problems; he offered a shrewd analysis of the interplay between money and morality in drama and expressed interest in the possibility of new kind of heroine with 'a man's seriousness' (quoted in Meyer, *Ibsen*, 1985, p. 380). Brandes offered the isolated Ibsen both friendship and an insight into the wider currents of European literature. He was aware that the long process of writing *Emperor and Galilean* was a rite of passage during which Ibsen's mind was formulating the prose theatre of the future; but he may not have recognised that his own input was a vital part of it.

THEATRICAL INFLUENCES

Ibsen's work in the theatre – he directed more than seventy plays by Eugène Scribe or in his style – had taught him practical skills. He knew how actors worked, and how the theatrical space available influenced the way a play could be made. With his lively and dynamic mother-in-law Magdalene Thoresen working for the theatre as translator of the French texts, he was also closely engaged in discussing plays at the level of language and structure. However, it would be hard to overestimate the impact of the Saxe-Meiningen Company and his subsequent friendship with Duke Georg II, which touched his imagination more profoundly than any fictional or critical work. There were no stars. The company was an ensemble where even the smallest roles were given a distinct character, just as Ibsen portrayed the servants in *A Doll's House* as individuals. Instead of the flapping backcloths lit by flickering chandeliers that Ibsen had coped with in Bergen, they incorporated materials such as metal and stone; the solidity of their sets paved the way for the **realism** of the Helmer household. Now that Ibsen was aware of a theatre company with acting skills and artistic vision perfectly suited to his **naturalistic** style, *The Pillars of Society* (1877) and the plays which followed no longer constituted a leap in the dark.

CONTEXT

Duke Georg II of Saxe-Meiningen (1826–1914), known as 'the theatre duke', married Helene Freifrau von Heldburg, one of the leading actresses of his company. There is still a ducal house of Saxe-Meiningen with links to the British and Dutch royal families.

CONTEXT

As well as a major theatre company Georg II sponsored an orchestra and was a close friend of Johannes Brahms (1833–97) and Richard Wagner (1813–83). He tried to curb German expansionism at the close of the nineteenth century, but his funeral took place on the day the Sarajevo assassination precipitated the First World War in June 1914.

IBSEN'S INFLUENCE

Naturalistic theatre burgeoned in late nineteenth-century Europe and there was a strong relationship between the new figure of the theatre director and the playwright. While the director could transmit his vision of theatre as a slice of life to the actor and designer, it was the writer who provided scripts exploring contemporary language and situations. In 1887 the clerk of a gas company, André Antoine (1858–1943), founded the Théâtre Libre in Paris specifically in order to stage Zola and Ibsen. The budget was so tiny that he borrowed furniture for the sets from his mother's house, and friends delivered the publicity leaflets by hand. But he rapidly attracted subscribers who wanted to be the first to experience a theatre in which, as Antoine put it, 'Returning a pencil or tipping over a cup will be as significant … as the grandiloquent excesses of the romantic theatre' (quoted in J. L. Styan, *Modern Drama in Theory and Practice: Realism and Naturalism*, 1981, p. 35). He went further than the Saxe-Meiningen Company in rejecting footlights and building his sets like real rooms with the **fourth wall** removed. He staged *The Wild Duck* and *Ghosts*, playing Oswald himself, and introduced a host of new writers. The most significant, Eugène Brieux (1858–1932), was profoundly influenced by Ibsen, challenging the censor with naturalistic plays on social issues such as *Damaged Goods* (1901), which depicts the social consequences of syphilis.

Antoine also staged works by a Scandinavian with an unwilling debt to Ibsen, August Strindberg (1849–1912). Both writers had experienced poverty, censorship and exile, and in his early career Strindberg was willing to consider translating *Love's Comedy*. However, his studies of sexual aggression – *The Father* (1887), about a man falling into madness as his wife torments him that their child is not his; and *Miss Julie* (1888), about a doomed sexual encounter between an aristocratic young girl and a servant – were savage reactions to what he considered the 'feminism' of Ibsen. During a period of intense mental illness Strindberg became convinced that Ibsen had based the suicidal poet Lovborg in *Hedda Gabler* on him in order to drive him to suicide – but, he added, he would 'stick that gun in the old troll's [Ibsen's] neck!' (quoted in Michael Meyer, *Ibsen*, 1985, p. 675). Like Ibsen, Strindberg shifted

 CHECK THE NET
A thoughtful article by Michael Billington comparing Ibsen and Strindberg as vital forces in modern theatre was published in the *Guardian* (15 February 2003). Visit **www. guardian.co.uk** and search for 'The troll in the drawing room'.

CHECK THE FILM
It is worth comparing some scenes from *A Doll's House* with Strindberg's *Miss Julie*. There are several films of this play, the most recent directed by Mike Figgis with Saffron Burrows in the role of Julie and Peter Mullan in the role of Jean (1999).

away from naturalism in later years, but his preface to *Miss Julie* pushes out from Zola to discuss the need to demonstrate on stage the complexity of human **motivation**. The misogyny of the play, in stark contrast to *A Doll's House*, is an interesting comment on naturalism: the naturalists were not as 'objective' as they liked to think.

The most developed techniques of theatrical naturalism emerged from the Moscow Art Theatre, founded by Vladimir Nemirovich-Danchenko (1858–1943) and Konstantin Stanislavsky (1863–1938) in 1898. These were not fully articulated by Stanislavsky until after the death of the playwright with whom their work is most closely associated, Anton Chekhov (1860–1904). A prolific writer of short stories before he turned to the stage, Chekhov found that Ibsen still retained too much of the **well-made play** format. He dismissed *Hedda Gabler* as sensationalist, for example; several of his own characters use a revolver, as Hedda does, but typically they fail to shoot themselves or anyone else and the overall tone of the plays is a mixture of quiet despair and political optimism. However, Ibsen had provided Stanislavsky himself with a successful acting role, Dr Stockmann in *An Enemy of the People*, and it was through reflections on this performance that he began to evolve the 'system' by which naturalistic actors have been taught ever since, learning to achieve an intense focus on their characters' desires and shutting out awareness of anything beyond the fourth wall.

In an England where the censor made life difficult for the serious dramatist, the reputation of *A Doll's House* made it a titillating prospect to the commercial theatre, and one person who seized the opportunity to benefit was Henry Arthur Jones (1851–1929), later to become one of the best-known West End playwrights. Offered Henry Herman's rough translation of *A Doll's House* and the opportunity to make it 'sympathetic', he produced *Breaking a Butterfly* (1884). Nora becomes the giddy young Flossie; Krogstad the 'thorough-paced scoundrel' and sexual predator Dunkley; and Flossie's husband, Humphrey Goddard, performs the 'miracle' Nora longs for by telling Dunkley he was the forger: 'Yes – I! Now do your worst to me. You shall not touch a hair of her head.' Krogstad's redemptive act of destroying the note of hand is given to

QUESTION

The Stanislavsky system requires the actor to be aware of his or her character's 'super-objective', the desire that motivates them and shapes their actions throughout the play. What 'super-objectives' can you detect in Nora and Helmer? How might you reveal them in action?

CONTEXT

In his old age Jones remarked that *A Doll's House* should end with Helmer 'pouring himself a stiff glass of whisky and water and lifting it reverently toward heaven exclaim[ing] "Thank God I'm well rid of her"' (quoted in Anthony Jenkins, *The Making of Victorian Drama*, 1991, p. 278).

CHECK THE BOOK
You can read an analysis of both *A Doll's House* and *Breaking a Butterfly* in Michael Mangan's *Staging Masculinities: History, Gender, Performance* (2002).

CONTEXT
Dublin-born Shaw's career as a playwright began with *Widowers' Houses* (first performed in 1892). A feminist and socialist, he was an early supporter and imitator of Ibsen. His later works include *Heartbreak House* (1919) and *Saint Joan* (1923). He is best remembered today for *Pygmalion* (1913), which formed the basis of the musical *My Fair Lady* (1956). Shaw is the only writer to have won both the Nobel Prize in Literature (in 1925) and an Oscar (for the 1938 film of *Pygmalion*).

another character altogether, and most bizarrely of all Dr Rank becomes the hearty Dan Birdseye, who wants to 'kick the fellow downstairs'. Flossie, of course, never walks out of the front door; instead the thwarted Dunkley does so while her husband proclaims: 'Flossie was a child yesterday: today she is a woman' (*Breaking a Butterfly*, Jones and Herman, 1884, p. 76). The play wholeheartedly endorses the institution of marriage, ending with the engagement of jolly Dan Birdseye to Flossie's sister. Jones grew to be somewhat ashamed of *Breaking a Butterfly*, however, and the copy in the British Library is marked 'not to be played ANYWHERE without the special written permission of the authors'.

Meanwhile, it was non-commercial managements, like that of J. T. Grein (1862–1935), that paved the way for Ibsen's real impact. Dutch by birth, Grein ran the Independent Theatre, one of the most influential theatre societies which – because it had the status of a private club – gave audiences a chance to encounter Ibsen and Zola despite the censor. Grein also approached George Bernard Shaw (1856–1950), then a novelist and critic, for a play. Shaw, who played Krogstad to the Nora of Eleanor Marx in an informal reading of *A Doll's House* in 1886, responded with *Widowers' Houses*, an attack on slum landlords, establishing himself as a political radical and **realist** playwright in the Ibsen tradition. His *Candida* (first performed in 1897) joined the Independent Theatre repertory as it was touring with *A Doll's House*. Exposing the sexual politics of a marriage in which a woman stays because of her husband's weakness, not her need, *Candida* is *A Doll's House*'s comedic complement. Shaw's play about prostitution, *Mrs Warren's Profession* (written in 1893 but refused a licence), proved as controversial as *Ghosts* when eventually staged privately in 1902. Harley Granville-Barker (1877–1946), whose own plays, such as *Waste* (1907), about abortion and political scandal, dealt with social issues in a restrained style closer to Ibsen than the effervescent Shaw, took over the Royal Court Theatre with his colleague J. E. Vedrenne in 1904 and developed an acting style that freed English actors from staginess and equipped them to work with Ibsen and his successors. He aimed to present the journey of the characters through the play rather than treating the action as a series of **points**, or 'big moments' to be milked for a round of applause.

It would be difficult to find a serious writer of plays in the nineteenth century who did *not* in some way acknowledge a debt to Ibsen. **Naturalism** is now so closely woven into the fabric of modern theatre that it is rarely possible to trace his direct influence. However, Arthur Miller (1915–2005) explicitly acknowledged him as a model for the way he showed the inextricable relationship between social issues and personal relationships. Miller's play *All My Sons* (1947, winner of the New York Drama Critics' Circle Award) closely resembles the social plays of Ibsen with a solidly constructed story about a pillar of society with a guilty secret. Joe Keller has sold defective aircraft during the war and blamed his business partner for it, and this poisons the lives of all those he loves. Central to the play is the **symbol** of the apple tree planted in memory of his pilot son Larry, which splits and falls as the secret begins to emerge.

In Britain the first play shaped by the new energies in the theatre that gathered to a head in 1956 was perceived to be John Osborne's *Look Back in Anger*. While other plays might lay claim to more originality, it seems fitting that the flagship of the new movement should have been a play using the typical Ibsenite blend of contemporary politics and well-made form, in Granville-Barker's old theatre, the Royal Court. Osborne's portrait of a marriage disintegrating under the pressures of 1950s England pays conscious homage to *A Doll's House* as the characters retreat from strife into a fantasy game of 'bears and squirrels'. If Osborne's Jimmy Porter was as hidebound by gender conventions as Helmer, others would subsequently challenge him and even reach out to the more innovative, non-naturalistic forms of which Ibsen was also a pioneer.

> **CONTEXT**
>
> Miller translated Ibsen's *An Enemy of the People* (it was staged in 1950) and paid him the following tribute in his preface to the published edition: 'There is one quality in Ibsen that no serious writer can afford to overlook. … It is his insistence, his utter conviction, that he is going to say what he has to say, and that the audience, by God, is going to listen. … Every Ibsen play begins with the unwritten words: "Now listen here!"'

World events	Henrik Ibsen's life	Literary events
1814 Denmark cedes Norway to Sweden in Treaty of Kiel		
		1815 Eugène Scribe begins writing plays
	1825 Marichen Altenburg marries Knud Ibsen	
1828 Central German Customs Union founded	**1828** Born in Skien on 20 March	**1828** Leo Tolstoy born
	1835 Knud Ibsen loses the family home	
1836 Mexican troops take the Alamo		**1836** Nikolai Gogol, *The Government Inspector*
1837 Accession of Queen Victoria; first daguerreotype image produced		**1837–8** Charles Dickens, *Oliver Twist*
1843 Ohm's law of sonic vibration discovered	**1843** Family moves to small farmhouse	**1843** Søren Kierkegaard, *Either/Or: A Fragment of Life*; Edvard Grieg born; Theatre Regulation Act
1844 Oskar I crowned king of Sweden and Norway	**1844** Apprenticed to pharmacist in Grimstad	**1844** Alexandre Dumas (Dumas *père*), *The Three Musketeers*
1845 Karl Marx expelled from France		**1845** Richard Wagner, *Tannhäuser*
1846 D. O. Hill takes first photographic portraits	**1846** Illegitimate son, Hans Jacob Henriksen, born	

World events	Henrik Ibsen's life	Literary events
1847 Ignaz Semmelweis discovers infections that lead to infant mortality		**1847** Charlotte Brontë, *Jane Eyre*; Emily Brontë, *Wuthering Heights*
1848 Revolutions in France and Italy; Marcus Thrane's uprising		**1848** Karl Marx and Friedrich Engels, *The Communist Manifesto*
1849 Gold rush in California	**1849** Poem 'In Autumn' published; writes *Catiline*	**1849** August Strindberg born
		1849–50 Charles Dickens, *David Copperfield*
1850 12,000 employed in factories in Norway	**1850** Moves to Kristiania; *Catiline* published under pseudonym; edits *Andhrimner*; *The Warrior's Barrow* performed (revised version published 1854)	**1850** Nathaniel Hawthorne, *The Scarlet Letter*
1851 Exhibition at Crystal Palace, Hyde Park	**1851** Starts as assistant director in Bergen	**1851** Herman Melville, *Moby-Dick*
1852 First airship flight over Paris	**1852** Trip to Denmark and Germany	**1852** Death of Nikolai Gogol
1853 Giuseppe Mazzini leads uprising in Milan against Austrian rule	**1853** *St John's Night* is staged	**1853** Elizabeth Gaskell, *Ruth*
1854 Britain enters Crimean War; loss of the Light Brigade		**1854** Charles Dickens, *Hard Times*
		1854–62 Coventry Patmore, *The Angel in the House*
1855 Telegraph network begun in Norway	**1855** *Lady Inger* is staged (published in 1857)	**1855** Walt Whitman, *Leaves of Grass*

World events

1856 Crimean War ends

1857 UK Matrimonial Causes Act establishes secular divorce in England

1859 Karl XV crowned king of Sweden and Norway; work begins on Suez Canal

1861 American Civil War begins; Édouard Manet exhibits in Paris

1862 Otto von Bismarck becomes prime minister of Prussia

1864 UK Contagious Diseases Act; war over Schleswig-Holstein

1865 President Abraham Lincoln assassinated in USA; Claude Monet exhibits in Paris

Henrik Ibsen's life

1856 *The Feast at Solhaug* is staged; becomes engaged to Suzannah Thoresen

1857 *Olaf Liljekrans* is staged; moves to Kristiania as artistic director

1858 Marries Suzannah Thoresen; *The Vikings at Helgeland* is performed

1859 Poems *In the Picture Gallery*; son Sigurd born

1861 Writes poem *Terje Vigen*

1862 *Love's Comedy* published (not performed until 1873)

1863 *The Pretenders* is published (first performed 1864)

1864 Moves to Rome

1865 Poem on death of Lincoln

Literary events

1856 Sigmund Freud and George Bernard Shaw born

1857 Gustave Flaubert, *Madame Bovary*

1859 Charles Darwin, *On the Origin of Species by Means of Natural Selection*

1860 Anton Chekhov born

1861 Death of Eugène Scribe

1862 Victor Hugo, *Les Misérables*

1863 Death of William Thackeray

1865–9 Leo Tolstoy, *War and Peace*

World events	Henrik Ibsen's life	Literary events
1866 First successful transatlantic telegraph cable; Alfred Nobel invents dynamite	**1866** *Brand* published	**1866** Fyodor Dostoevsky, *Crime and Punishment*; formation of Saxe-Meiningen Company
1867 Second Reform Act gives vote to some of male working class in UK	**1867** *Peer Gynt* published (not performed until 1876)	**1867** T. W. Robertson, *Caste*; Karl Marx, *Das Kapital* (first volume)
1868 San Francisco earthquake	**1868** Moves to Dresden	**1868** Wilkie Collins, *The Moonstone*
1869 Annual meeting of the Storting introduced in Norway	**1869** Mother dies; *The League of Youth*	**1869** John Stuart Mill, *On the Subjection of Women*
1870 UK Married Women's Property Act; start of Franco-Prussian War		**1870** Death of Charles Dickens
1871 Paris Commune	**1871** *Poems* published	**1871** Charles Darwin, *The Descent of Man*
		1871–2 George Eliot, *Middlemarch*
1872 Oskar II crowned king of Sweden and Norway		**1872–90** Georg Brandes, *Main Currents in Nineteenth Century Literature*
1873 Bank failures across USA	**1873** *Emperor and Galilean* published	**1873** Jules Verne, *Around the World in Eighty Days*
1874 About 45,000 now working in factories in Norway; Impressionist exhibition in Paris	**1874** Visits Norway	
1875 Norway begins major railways programme	**1875** Moves to Munich	**1875–8** Leo Tolstoy, *Anna Karenina*

World events

1876 Alexander Graham Bell invents telephone

1877 Thomas Edison invents phonograph

1878 Salvation Army founded in UK; first long-distance call made by Bell Telephone Company

1879 Thomas Edison invents electric light bulb; Pierre Auguste Renoir exhibits in Paris

1880 Amnesty for those who took part in Paris Commune of 1871

1881 President James Garfield assassinated in USA

1882 UK Married Women's Property Act; pogroms throughout Russia after assassination of Tsar Alexander II in previous year

Henrik Ibsen's life

1876 Lives mainly in Rome; meets Saxe-Meiningen Company

1877 Father dies; *The Pillars of Society* is staged; awarded honorary doctorate by University of Uppsala

1879 *A Doll's House* published and staged

1881 *Ghosts* published

1882 *Ghosts* is staged; *An Enemy of the People* published (first performed 1883)

Literary events

1876 First complete performance of Richard Wagner's *Ring* cycle

1877 Annie Besant and Charles Bradlaugh prosecuted for publishing Charles Knowlton's work on contraception, *The Fruits of Philosophy*

1878 James Whistler sues John Ruskin for a bad review of his painting *Nocturne in Black and Gold*

1880 Electric light in the theatre used for first time; Émile Zola, 'Naturalism in the Theatre'

1881 Henry James, *The Portrait of a Lady*; death of Fyodor Dostoevsky

1882 Death of Charles Darwin

1883 Death of Richard Wagner

World events

1884 Political parties established in Norway; divorce reintroduced in France under Third Republic

1885 Karl Benz makes first car, known as the horseless carriage

1886 Statue of Liberty erected; seven sentenced to death after anarchist bomb in Chicago

1887 Norwegian Labour Party formed

1888 George Eastman produces Kodak camera; Carl Gassner manufactures first dry cell batteries

1889 Eiffel Tower built

Henrik Ibsen's life

1884 *The Wild Duck* published (first performed 1885)

1885 First staging of *Brand*; visits Norway; moves to Munich

1886 *Rosmersholm* published (first performed 1887)

1887 Spends the summer in Jutland

1888 *The Lady from the Sea* published (first performed 1889)

1889 London and New York productions of *A Doll's House*

1890 *Hedda Gabler* published

1891 *Hedda Gabler* is staged; returns to Norway

Literary events

1884 Henry Arthur Jones, *Breaking a Butterfly*

1886 Robert Louis Stevenson, *The Strange Case of Dr Jekyll and Mr Hyde*; death of Franz Liszt

1887 André Antoine founds Théâtre Libre in Paris; August Strindberg, *The Father*

1888 August Strindberg, *Miss Julie*

1889 Gerhart Hauptmann, *Before Dawn*

1890 William James, *Principles of Psychology*; Oscar Wilde, *The Picture of Dorian Gray*

1891 Thomas Hardy, *Tess of the D'Urbervilles*; J. T. Grein founds Independent Theatre Club

World events	Henrik Ibsen's life	Literary events
	1892 *The Master Builder* is published; Sigurd marries Bergliot Bjørnson	**1892** Charlotte Perkins Gilman, 'The Yellow Wallpaper'; Eugène Brieux, *Monsieur de Réboval*; George Bernard Shaw, *Widowers' Houses*
1893 UK Married Women's Property Act	**1893** Birth of grandson Tancred	**1893** George Bernard Shaw writes *Mrs Warren's Profession* but censor refuses to give it a licence; Oscar Wilde's *A Woman of No Importance* staged
1894 Lumière brothers invent the cinematograph	**1894** *Little Eyolf* published (first performed 1895)	**1894** Sarah Grand coins the term 'New Woman'
1895 Wilhelm Röntgen discovers X-rays; London School of Economics and Political Science founded	**1895** Moves back to Kristiania	**1895** Thomas Hardy, *Jude the Obscure*
1896 Olympic Games revived after 1,500 years	**1896** *John Gabriel Borkman* published (first performed 1897)	**1896** Anton Chekhov, *The Seagull*; Alfred Jarry, *Ubu Roi*
1897 Rudolf Diesel demonstrates first compression-ignition engine; Guglielmo Marconi makes first communication by wireless signals		
1898 Franchise extended to all Norwegian males	**1898** Seventieth birthday celebrations	**1898** Stanislavsky co-founds Moscow Art Theatre
		1898–1901 August Strindberg, *To Damascus* (trilogy)

World events

1899–1902 Boer War

1900 First Zeppelin flight

1901 Death of Queen Victoria; first Nobel Prizes awarded

1903 Orville and Wilbur Wright make their first flight

1904 Trans-Siberian railway opens

1905 Union between Norway and Sweden dissolved; Haakon VII crowned king of Norway; bourgeois revolution in Moscow

1906 Ivan Pavlov discovers conditioned reflexes; Fauvists exhibit in Paris

Henrik Ibsen's life

1899 *When We Dead Awaken* published (first performed 1900); Sigurd made head of Norwegian Foreign Ministry

1900 First stroke

1901 Second stroke

1903 Bust of Ibsen sculpted by Stephen Sinding; third stroke

1905 Sigurd's political career ends and he comes to live near his father

1906 Dies on 23 May

Literary events

1899 Anton Chekhov's *Uncle Vanya* staged; Noël Coward born

1900 Giacomo Puccini's *Tosca* staged

1901 Sigmund Freud, *The Interpretation of Dreams*

1902 Death of Émile Zola; August Strindberg, *A Dream Play*

1903 John Synge, *In the Shadow of the Glen*

1904 Anton Chekhov, *The Cherry Orchard*; death of Chekhov

1905 Edward Gordon Craig, *The Art of the Theatre*

PLAYS BY IBSEN

The Collected Works of Henrik Ibsen, trans. William Archer, Heinemann, 1906–12
Produced in twelve volumes, Archer's translations have also been reprinted individually and collectively many times since first published

Plays: One, trans. Michael Meyer, Methuen, 1980
Ghosts, included in this collection, explores what happens to a wife who stays in a troubled marriage

Plays: Two, trans. Michael Meyer, Methuen, 1980
You may find it interesting to read Meyer's translation of *A Doll's House* in this collection and compare it with Peter Watts's 1965 translation; *An Enemy of the People* shows the social reformer Ibsen that attracted disciples like Shaw; *Hedda Gabler* develops the theme of marriage

Six Plays by Henrik Ibsen, trans. Eva Le Gallienne, Modern Library, 1951
Le Gallienne's translation of *A Doll's House*, included in this volume, is notable for the omission of the silk stockings scene

An Enemy of the People, adapted by Arthur Miller, Nick Hern Books, 1989
This version by the award-winning playwright Miller was first staged in 1950 and published the following year

Peer Gynt, trans. Michael Meyer, Methuen, 1973
Ibsen in a different vein which shows his poetic and epic strengths

WIDER READING

For connections and comparisons with *A Doll's House* see the relevant pages of these Notes (provided in bold below):

DRAMA
Arthur Miller, *Plays: One*, Methuen, 1988
All My Sons (first published in 1947) is included in this collection **(p. 111)**

John Osborne, *Look Back in Anger*, Penguin, 1982
Osborne's play was first performed in 1956 **(p. 111)**

Friedrich Schiller, *Plays Two*, trans. Robert David MacDonald, Oberon Books, 2005
> *Don Carlos*, a tragedy in five acts, was originally published and performed in 1787; it is a good example of a Romantic play and is one of two plays published in this collection **(p. 8)**

For a varied examination of the sexual politics of the nineteenth century and early twentieth century, the following works are an interesting selection:

J. M. Barrie, *Collected Plays*, Hodder & Stoughton, 1948
> Although now best remembered for *Peter Pan*, Barrie wrote a number of well-received plays, including *The Twelve-Pound Look* (published in this collection), first published in 1910 **(p. 59)**

Harley Granville-Barker, *Plays: One*, Methuen, 1993
> Includes *Waste*, banned in 1907 by the Lord Chamberlain **(p. 110)**

George Bernard Shaw, *Plays Pleasant*, Penguin, 2003
> *Candida* (first performed in 1897) is published in this collection **(p. 110)**

George Bernard Shaw, *Plays Unpleasant*, Penguin, 2000
> *Widowers' Houses* (1892) and *Mrs Warren's Profession* (written in 1893) are both published in this collection **(pp. 78, 110)**

August Strindberg, *Five Plays*, trans Harry G. Carlson, Signet, 1984
> *Miss Julie* (1888) is included in this collection **(p. 108)**

Oscar Wilde, *Complete Works of Oscar Wilde*, ed. Merlin Holland, Collins, 1994 (fifth edition 2003)
> *The Importance of Being Earnest* was first performed in 1895 **(p. 10)**

VICTORIAN AND NINETEENTH-CENTURY PROSE AND POETRY
Charlotte Brontë, *Jane Eyre*, 1847 **(p. 37)**

Emily Brontë, *Wuthering Heights*, 1847 **(p. 98)**

Robert Browning, *Complete Poetic and Dramatic Works*, 1895 **(p. 44)**

Samuel Butler, *Erewhon*, 1872 **(p. 13)**

Charles Dickens, *David Copperfield*, 1849–50 **(pp. 54, 104)**

Fyodor Dostoevsky, *Crime and Punishment*, 1866 **(p. 104)**

George Eliot, *Middlemarch*, 1871–2 **(p. 105)**

Gustave Flaubert, *Madame Bovary*, 1857 **(p. 105)**

Elizabeth Gaskell, *Ruth*, 1853 **(p. 30)**

Madame de Staël, *Corinne*, 1807 **(p. 51)**

Alfred Tennyson, *The Princess*, 1847 **(p. 102)**

Leo Tolstoy, *Anna Karenina*, 1875–8 **(p. 56)**

Leo Tolstoy, *War and Peace*, 1865–9 **(p. 105)**

Émile Zola, *Thérèse Raquin*, 1867 **(p. 101)**

MODERN NOVELS

A. S. Byatt, *The Biographer's Tale*, 2000 **(p. 27)**

Matthew Kneale, *English Passengers*, 2000 **(p. 101)**

BIOGRAPHY

Robert Ferguson, *Henrik Ibsen: A New Biography*, Richard Cohen Books, 1996
Contains hitherto undiscovered material and offers details of Ibsen's personal life and development

Halvdan Koht, *The Life of Ibsen*, trans. and ed. Einar Haugen and A. E. Santaniello, Benjamin Blom, 1971
First published in 1928

Michael Meyer, *Ibsen*, Penguin, 1985
Abridged version of Meyer's detailed three-volume biography (published between 1967 and 1971); a valuable study of the development of Ibsen as a writer

ON NATURALISTIC ACTING

The following titles contain careful exposition of an actor's training for the **naturalistic** Ibsen style and offer a useful vocabulary with which to discuss performance and helpful advice for anyone attempting it:

Konstantin Stanislavsky, *An Actor Prepares*, trans. Elizabeth Hapgood, Methuen, 1979

Konstantin Stanislavsky, *Building a Character*, trans. Elizabeth Hapgood, Methuen, 1979

Konstantin Stanislavsky, *Creating a Role*, trans. Elizabeth Hapgood, Methuen, 1979

Lee Strasberg, *A Dream of Passion: The Development of the Method*, Bloomsbury, 1988

ON WRITING PLAYS

William Archer, *Play-Making*, Chapman and Hall, 1912

Draws extensively on his experience as translator of Ibsen; it has been reprinted as recently as 2006 by Dodo Press

George Pierce Baker, *Dramatic Technique*, Da Capo Press, 1976

The workshop manual, first published in 1919, for Baker's class that included Eugene O'Neill

Toby Cole (ed.), *Playwrights on Playwriting*, Methuen, 1988

Includes George Bernard Shaw, William Archer, Émile Zola, Anton Chekhov and August Strindberg, and contains Ibsen's scenario for *A Doll's House*

IBSEN AND HIS HEIRS

Edvard Beyer, *Ibsen: The Man and His Work*, trans. M. Wells, Hammer Press, 1978

A Norwegian perspective with many photographs, including some from the original productions of the plays

Harold Clurman, *Ibsen*, Macmillan, 1977

A director's view of some of the major plays with some useful theatrical insights

Michael Egan, *Ibsen: The Critical Heritage*, Routledge & Kegan Paul, 1972

Contains reviews from first British productions, including several essays by William Archer and noted Victorian writers such as Henry James and Edmund Gosse

Ronald Gray, *Ibsen: A Dissenting View*, Cambridge University Press, 1977

Sums up the main arguments against Ibsen since the 1950s

Daniel Haakonsen (ed.), *Contemporary Approaches to Ibsen: International Seminar Proceedings*, Universitetsforlaget, 1965

A series of lectures in celebration of Ibsen by international scholars

Anthony Jenkins, *The Making of Victorian Drama*, Cambridge University Press, 1991
Examines the impact of Ibsen in Britain and on the tentative exploration towards greater realism in the commercial theatre

James McFarlane (ed.), *The Cambridge Companion to Ibsen*, Cambridge University Press, 1994
This collection of essays has a useful general introduction as well as a detailed bibliography

Michael Mangan, *Staging Masculinities: History, Gender, Performance*, Palgrave Macmillan, 2002
Discusses the construction of masculinity in the theatre and explores in detail both *A Doll's House* and *Breaking a Butterfly*

Frederick J. Marker and Lise-Lone Marker, *Ibsen's Lively Art: A Performance Study of the Major Plays*, Cambridge University Press, 1989
Explores Ibsen in the theatre and discusses contrasting versions of *A Doll's House* among other plays

Toril Moi, *Henrik Ibsen and the Birth of Modernism: Art, Theater, Philosophy*, Oxford University Press, 2006
Innovative study which reappraises Ibsen's role in literary history; Moi offers a detailed examination of *A Doll's House* and an extremely original discussion of Ibsen's visual imagination

Elizabeth Robins, *Ibsen and the Actress*, Hogarth Press, 1928
Pamphlet describing the impact of Ibsen on her artistic and political life; it was reprinted in 1973 by Haskell House Publishers

George Bernard Shaw, *The Quintessence of Ibsenism*, Constable and Company, 1932
Originally written for a Fabian Society meeting in 1890, and first published in 1891

J. L. Styan, *Modern Drama in Theory and Practice: Realism and Naturalism*, Cambridge University Press, 1981
Puts Ibsen in the context of naturalistic theatre in general and assesses his influence on practitioners such as André Antoine

Joan Templeton, *Ibsen's Women*, Cambridge University Press, 2001
Explores Ibsen's relationships with women and the influence of figures such as Magdalene Thoresen on the plays; a useful feminist reading of *A Doll's House*

Egil Törnqvist, *A Doll's House*, Cambridge University Press, 1995
Discusses productions in all media, including film, radio and the stage, and also addresses some of the problems of translating Ibsen

Raymond Williams, *Drama from Ibsen to Brecht*, Pelican, 1976
Highly influential study which explores the limits of **naturalism**; Williams is perhaps the most noted literary theorist to engage with Ibsen in the later twentieth century

GENERAL

Peter Ackroyd, *Dickens*, Sinclair-Stevenson, 1990
A lively and very readable biography of one of the most popular and influential Victorian writers, whom Ibsen read and admired

George J. Becker (ed.), *Documents of Modern Literary Realism*, Princeton University Press, 1963
Includes Émile Zola's important essay on naturalism in the theatre

Eric Bentley (ed.), *The Theory of the Modern Stage: An Introduction to Modern Theatre and Drama*, Penguin, 1982
Includes the 1871 lecture by Georg Brandes attended and admired by Ibsen

Georg Brandes, *Main Currents in Nineteenth Century Literature*, 1872–90
All six volumes have been reprinted as recently as 2006 by Kessinger Publishing

Judith Butcher, *Gender Trouble: Feminism and the Subversion of Identity*, Routledge, 1990
A difficult but rewarding study of how people perform their gender

Margaret Drabble (ed.), *The Oxford Companion to English Literature*, Oxford University Press, revised sixth edition, 2006
A valuable general reference guide

Terry Eagleton, *Literary Theory: An Introduction*, Blackwell, 1983
Sketches the history of literary criticism; revised in 1996

Martin Esslin, *The Field of Drama: How the Signs of Drama Create Meaning on Stage and Screen*, Methuen, 1987
Straightforward and readable guide to theatre semiotics

Lesley Ferris, *Acting Women: Images of Women in Theatre*, Macmillan, 1990
The chapter 'The Wilful Woman' is useful in considering *A Doll's House*

James Greenwood, *The Seven Curses of London*, Kessinger Publishing, 2005
Originally published in 1869, it is possible to read it online at **www.victorianlondon.org** – click on 'Publications' and 'Social Investigation/Journalism' to find the full text

Tyrone Guthrie, *A Life in the Theatre*, Columbus Books, 1987
Autobiography of the renowned Shakespearean director; first published in 1959

Richard Jacobs, *A Beginner's Guide to Critical Reading: Readings for Students*, Routledge, 2001
An entertaining and informative introduction

Jerome K. Jerome, *Stage-Land*, Chatto & Windus, 1889
This short but entertaining read has been reprinted as recently as 2007 by Dodo Press

Francis O'Gorman (ed.), *Victorian Literature and Finance*, Oxford University Press, 2007
Contains Jane Moody's essay 'The Drama of Capital: Risk, Belief, and Liability on the Victorian Stage' (Chapter 5, pp. 91–110)

Susie Orbach, *Fat Is a Feminist Issue*, Hamlyn, 1979
Explores the connection between sexual politics and female attitudes towards food and diet

Michael Patterson, *The Oxford Dictionary of Plays*, Oxford University Press, 2005
Gives brief summaries and useful information on many of the plays discussed in these Notes

George Bernard Shaw, *Our Theatres in the Nineties*, Constable, 1948
A collection of insightful theatrical articles and reviews written by Shaw when drama critic for the *Saturday Review* from 1895 to 1898; this collection was originally published in three volumes in 1932

Sheila Stowell, *A Stage of Their Own: Feminist Playwrights of the Suffrage Era*, Manchester University Press, 1992
In this detailed study Stowell examines Ibsen's influence on British Edwardian women playwrights

J. L. Styan, *The Dark Comedy: The Development of Modern Comic Tragedy*, Cambridge University Press, 1962 (second edition 1968)
Discusses the blending of **comedy** and **tragedy** in theatre; Styan updated and revised his work for the second edition

John Russell Taylor, *The Rise and Fall of the Well Made Play*, Methuen, 1967
Discusses the development of the **well-made play** both before and after the impact of Ibsen

Mick Wallis and Simon Shepherd, *Studying Plays*, Arnold, 1998
Excellent introduction to theatre studies with much detail on *A Doll's House*

allusion a passing reference in a work of literature to something outside the text; may include other works of literature, myth, historical facts or biographical detail

ambiguous having the capacity to have double, multiple or uncertain meanings

aside when a character speaks in such a way that some or all of the other characters on the stage cannot hear what is being said; or they address the audience directly. It is a device used to reveal a character's private thoughts, emotions and intentions

body language how people show their feelings and emotions by the way they move, sit or stand – often revealing that these are different from those which they are expressing in words

cliché a widely used expression which, through overuse, has lost impact and originality

colloquial everyday speech used by people in informal situations

comedy a story with a happy ending, most commonly, but not exclusively, used of plays

confidant, confidante a **stock character** whose function is to listen to the confidences and intentions of the **protagonist**

denouement the point in the play where the whole plot has finally unfolded (from the French for 'untying a knot')

development and complication the central section of a **well-made play** which makes the situation more complex and creates **suspense** about the outcome

dialect a manner of speaking or form of language peculiar to an individual or particular region or class; it differs from the standard language of a country

double take a comic technique where the actor does not instantly react to a shock, and then suddenly realises what has occurred

drag act a performance in the clothes of the opposite sex, such as that of a pantomime dame, traditionally played by a man

dramatic monologue a poetic form in which there is one speaker – not the poet – addressing the reader

duologue a scene or part of a scene between two characters

Enlightenment term used to describe a literary and philosophical movement in Europe beginning in the late seventeenth century and continuing for most of the eighteenth century, and characterised by a firm faith in the powers of human reason

eponymous adjective describing the character who gives his or her name to the title of a play or novel

euphemism an inoffensive word or phrase substituted for one considered offensive or hurtful

existentialism the idea that we are shaped by the choices that we make rather than possessing innate qualities

exposition the opening of a play in which all the information that the audience needs in order to understand the situation is put over. In a **well-made play** the playwright tries to do this without making the fact obvious

foil character whose main function is to provide a contrast to the central figure

fourth wall **naturalistic** plays are often set in rooms; effectively, one 'wall' of these rooms is removed, allowing the audience to look in. Occasionally an actor might face the audience while looking into an imaginary mirror or fire, something that might be present on the 'wall'

hegemony term coined by the Marxist philosopher Antonio Gramsci; it means that a diverse culture can be ruled or dominated by one group or class

ideology shared beliefs of a culture which are taken for granted and thus never questioned

imagery descriptive language which uses images to make actions, objects and characters more vivid in the reader's mind. **Metaphors** and **similes** are examples of imagery

imperative voice the way a verb is inflected to express command

ingénue term for the innocent young heroine of the play; nineteenth- and early twentieth-century companies would employ an actress who specialised in such roles

irony incongruity between what might be expected and what actually happens; the ill-timed arrival of an event that had been hoped for; the humorous or sarcastic use of words to imply the opposite of what they normally mean

melodrama popular theatrical genre of the nineteenth century. Distinguished by moralistic plots – often rooted in class struggle – with sensational effects. Music played an important role; originally it was used to evade the licensing laws which made it difficult for theatres to stage spoken drama, but it became important as a device to heighten the emotion of climactic moments

metaphor a figure of speech in which a word or phrase is applied to an object, a character or an action which does not literally belong to it, in order to imply a resemblance and create an unusual or striking image in the reader's mind

metatheatre a term used to describe drama about drama; metatheatrical plays openly draw attention to their theatricality by the use of such devices as **asides** and **soliloquies**, role playing and songs. Plays within plays are also implicitly metatheatrical

modernism cultural shift during the decades just before and after the First World War. Modernists rejected traditional forms of art and literature in order to confront the new social and political aspects of an industrialised world in which values were changing

motivation the desires and intentions that drive characters in **naturalistic** drama to behave as they do

narrative story, tale or any recital of events, and the manner in which it is told

naturalistic, naturalism theatrical style which tries to create the illusion of reality on the stage. The actors do not address the audience, but behave as if they are unaware of them; the language and situations are intended to be credible and **realistic**; and the settings mirror the real world as closely as possible

paradox seemingly absurd or self-contradictory statement that is or may be true

parody imitation of a work of literature or a literary style designed to ridicule the original

patriarchy a society where the authority and ideas of men dominate over those of women

point a moment at which an actor might pause to let the audience register a moment of high emotion

practical term for **properties** and items of stage furniture which actually fulfil their function, as opposed to painted images

properties, props objects used in the play, some of which may be important to the action, such as Krogstad's letter

proscenium arch frame around the stage in theatres built during the nineteenth and early twentieth centuries. It marks the edge of the **fourth wall**. In Ibsen's time the frame extended round all four sides of this 'wall' like a picture frame, although the bottom border later disappeared. This form of stage is associated with **naturalism**

protagonist the central character whose actions form the focus of the play

raisonneur a detached observer who comments on the action – generally a professional man, often a doctor, like Rank

realism literary portrayal of the 'real' world, in both physical and psychological detail, rather than an imaginary or ideal one. Victorian novels sometimes described themselves in this way

reification Marxist term meaning the making of human beings into commodities

resolution final moments of a play in which the loose ends are tied up

reversal of expectation a scene which surprises the audience by changing the whole course of the story or the balance of sympathy in the play

rhetoric structured and patterned language used in formal speech-making

Romantic movement rebellion against the scientific rationalism and aristocratically based social order of the earlier eighteenth century in favour of politically radical art forms grounded in spontaneous feeling and idealising nature

satire a type of literature in which folly, evil or topical issues are held up to scorn through ridicule, **irony** or exaggeration

scenario a detailed plan for a play

scène à faire term invented by French pioneers of the **well-made play** to indicate a crucial scene, usually a confrontation, which the audience would anticipate with excitement

simile a figure of speech which compares two things using the words 'like' or 'as'

soliloquy a dramatic device which allows a character alone on the stage to speak directly to the audience as if thinking aloud, revealing their inner thoughts, feelings and intentions

stage business non-verbal action on the stage, prescribed in the stage directions or added by an actor or the director

stock character the kind of character one could expect to see in a particular genre – for example the oppressed mother in a **melodrama**; the 'best friend' who listens to the confidences of the hero or heroine in a romantic **comedy**; the gossipy old woman who exists mainly to relay information to the audience in a **naturalistic** play

strong curtain a powerful line of dialogue or situation which occurs just before the fall of the curtain. Generally placed immediately before the last act of the play to maximise **suspense** about the outcome

subtext theatrical term to describe a pattern of emotions and energies that are not directly spoken about but show themselves through trivial actions or remarks which seem casual on the surface. It is a feature of **naturalistic** drama and Oscar Wilde was a pioneer of the technique in England

suspense excitement about the outcome of the story, often raised to a high pitch just before a break in the action

symbolic, symbolism investing material objects with abstract powers and meanings greater than their own; allowing a complex idea to be represented by a single object

tableau if the situation at the end of an act was particularly striking, Victorian actors would briefly 'freeze' to allow the audience to take in the stage picture

tragedy in its original sense, a drama dealing with elevated actions and emotions and characters of high social standing in which a terrible outcome becomes inevitable as a result of an unstoppable sequence of events and a fatal flaw in the personality of the **protagonist**. More recently, tragedy has come to include courses of events happening to ordinary individuals that are inevitable because of social and cultural conditions or natural disasters

villain character responsible for the troubles of the **protagonist**; a **stock character**

well-made play the form taken by most Victorian West End drama, derived from the French dramatists Eugène Scribe and Victorien Sardou. A well-made play has a clear structure: the **exposition** tells us what we need to know (usually that some of the characters have a secret); the **development and complication** bring the situation to crisis point, usually around the end of the penultimate act, as secrets come out and throw people into confusion; finally there is a **resolution**

AUTHOR OF THESE NOTES

Frances Gray is Reader in Drama at the University of Sheffield. She has written widely on theatre: her published books include titles on Noël Coward and women in the theatre. She is also a playwright, has a Radio Times award for comedy and is the author of the York Notes Advanced title *A Woman of No Importance*.

GCSE

Maya Angelou
I Know Why the Caged Bird Sings

Jane Austen
Pride and Prejudice

Alan Ayckbourn
Absent Friends

Elizabeth Barrett Browning
Selected Poems

Robert Bolt
A Man for All Seasons

Harold Brighouse
Hobson's Choice

Charlotte Brontë
Jane Eyre

Emily Brontë
Wuthering Heights

Brian Clark
Whose Life is it Anyway?

Robert Cormier
Heroes

Shelagh Delaney
A Taste of Honey

Charles Dickens
David Copperfield
Great Expectations
Hard Times
Oliver Twist
Selected Stories

Roddy Doyle
Paddy Clarke Ha Ha Ha

George Eliot
Silas Marner
The Mill on the Floss

Anne Frank
The Diary of a Young Girl

William Golding
Lord of the Flies

Oliver Goldsmith
She Stoops to Conquer

Willis Hall
The Long and the Short and the Tall

Thomas Hardy
Far from the Madding Crowd
The Mayor of Casterbridge
Tess of the d'Urbervilles
The Withered Arm and other Wessex Tales

L. P. Hartley
The Go-Between

Seamus Heaney
Selected Poems

Susan Hill
I'm the King of the Castle

Barry Hines
A Kestrel for a Knave

Louise Lawrence
Children of the Dust

Harper Lee
To Kill a Mockingbird

Laurie Lee
Cider with Rosie

Arthur Miller
The Crucible
A View from the Bridge

Robert O'Brien
Z for Zachariah

Frank O'Connor
My Oedipus Complex and Other Stories

George Orwell
Animal Farm

J. B. Priestley
An Inspector Calls
When We Are Married

Willy Russell
Educating Rita
Our Day Out

J. D. Salinger
The Catcher in the Rye

William Shakespeare
Henry IV Part I
Henry V
Julius Caesar
Macbeth
The Merchant of Venice
A Midsummer Night's Dream
Much Ado About Nothing
Romeo and Juliet
The Tempest
Twelfth Night

George Bernard Shaw
Pygmalion

Mary Shelley
Frankenstein

R. C. Sherriff
Journey's End

Rukshana Smith
Salt on the Snow

John Steinbeck
Of Mice and Men

Robert Louis Stevenson
Dr Jekyll and Mr Hyde

Jonathan Swift
Gulliver's Travels

Robert Swindells
Daz 4 Zoe

Mildred D. Taylor
Roll of Thunder, Hear My Cry

Mark Twain
Huckleberry Finn

James Watson
Talking in Whispers

Edith Wharton
Ethan Frome

William Wordsworth
Selected Poems

A Choice of Poets

Mystery Stories of the Nineteenth Century including The Signalman

Nineteenth Century Short Stories

Poetry of the First World War

Six Women Poets

For the AQA Anthology:
Duffy and Armitage & Pre-1914 Poetry
Heaney and Clarke & Pre-1914 Poetry
Poems from Different Cultures

Key Stage 3

William Shakespeare
Henry V
Macbeth
Much Ado About Nothing
Richard III
The Tempest

Margaret Atwood
Cat's Eye
The Handmaid's Tale
Jane Austen
Emma
Mansfield Park
Persuasion
Pride and Prejudice
Sense and Sensibility
William Blake
Songs of Innocence and of
Experience
The Brontës
Selected Poems
Charlotte Brontë
Jane Eyre
Villette
Emily Brontë
Wuthering Heights
Angela Carter
The Bloody Chamber
Nights at the Circus
Wise Children
Geoffrey Chaucer
The Franklin's Prologue and Tale
The Merchant's Prologue and
Tale
The Miller's Prologue and Tale
The Prologue to the Canterbury
Tales
The Pardoner's Tale
The Wife of Bath's Prologue and
Tale
Caryl Churchill
Top Girls
John Clare
Selected Poems
Joseph Conrad
Heart of Darkness
Charles Dickens
Bleak House
Great Expectations
Hard Times
Emily Dickinson
Selected Poems
Carol Ann Duffy
Selected Poems
The World's Wife
George Eliot
Middlemarch
The Mill on the Floss
T. S. Eliot
Selected Poems
The Waste Land

F. Scott Fitzgerald
The Great Gatsby
John Ford
'Tis Pity She's a Whore
E. M. Forster
A Passage to India
Michael Frayn
Spies
Charles Frazier
Cold Mountain
Brian Friel
Making History
Translations
William Golding
The Spire
Thomas Hardy
Jude the Obscure
The Mayor of Casterbridge
The Return of the Native
Selected Poems
Tess of the d'Urbervilles
Nathaniel Hawthorne
The Scarlet Letter
Seamus Heaney
Selected Poems from 'Opened
Ground'
Homer
The Iliad
The Odyssey
Aldous Huxley
Brave New World
Henrik Ibsen
A Doll's House
Kazuo Ishiguro
The Remains of the Day
James Joyce
Dubliners
John Keats
Selected Poems
Philip Larkin
High Windows
The Whitsun Weddings and
Selected Poems
Ian McEwan
Atonement
Christopher Marlowe
Doctor Faustus
Edward II
Arthur Miller
All My Sons
Death of a Salesman
John Milton
Paradise Lost Books I & II

Toni Morrison
Beloved
George Orwell
Nineteen Eighty-Four
Sylvia Plath
Selected Poems
William Shakespeare
Antony and Cleopatra
As You Like It
Hamlet
Henry IV Part I
King Lear
Macbeth
Measure for Measure
The Merchant of Venice
A Midsummer Night's Dream
Much Ado About Nothing
Othello
Richard II
Richard III
Romeo and Juliet
The Taming of the Shrew
The Tempest
Twelfth Night
The Winter's Tale
Mary Shelley
Frankenstein
Richard Brinsley Sheridan
The School for Scandal
Bram Stoker
Dracula
Alfred Tennyson
Selected Poems
Alice Walker
The Color Purple
John Webster
The Duchess of Malfi
The White Devil
Oscar Wilde
The Importance of Being
Earnest
A Woman of No Importance
Tennessee Williams
Cat on a Hot Tin Roof
The Glass Menagerie
A Streetcar Named Desire
Jeanette Winterson
Oranges Are Not the Only Fruit
Virginia Woolf
To the Lighthouse
William Wordsworth
The Prelude and Selected Poems
W. B. Yeats
Selected Poems
Poetry of the First World War